THE HERITAGE OF OUR FATHERS

(And Naboth said to Ahab, The Lord forbid it me, that I should give the inheritance of my fathers unto thee.—I Kings 21: 3)

The Free Church of Scotland: Her Origin and Testimony

by

G. N. M. Collins

Professor of Church History
in the
Free Church College, Edinburgh

THE KNOX PRESS
15 NORTH BANK STREET
EDINBURGH

1974

First published 1974

©

G. N. M. Collins

Printed by Lindsay & Co. Ltd., Edinburgh

INTRODUCTION

The purpose of this book is not only to provide a brief, up-to-date history of the Free Church of Scotland, but to show that, although circumstances compelled her at her formation as a separate denomination in 1843 to add the word "Free" to her denominational designation, she has maintained direct continuity with the pre-Disruption Church of Scotland in the Reformed tradition. She has not fallen out of sympathy with the evangelical Presbyterianism of Scotland either in principle or in doctrine; indeed, it was for the preservation of the inheritance which had come down to her from the Scottish Reformers that she took her separate stand in 1843. Her quarrel then was primarily with the State, which was denying her the spiritual independence guaranteed to her by successive enactments over the centuries. It was from a usurping government that she separated in 1843; and *that* disruption had as its unhappy consequence the rending asunder of the Church herself—the Free Church of Scotland choosing to relinquish the benefits of State establishment rather than lose her spiritual freedom; and the residuary Church of Scotland acquiescing in the enactments of a despotic Government the effect of which was to assign to the Established Church the degraded status of a mere department of State.

Some, no doubt, will regret the recalling of these—

> *old, unhappy, far-off things,*
> *and battles long ago*

but the Church which allows herself to forget the lessons of her history, and the hand of God in the shaping of her destiny is both unworthy of her high calling and regardless of her own safety. "Thou shalt remember all the way which the Lord thy God led thee" is as needful a caution for the people of God in this modern world as it was for Israel in the dawn of her history. "Forgetful Green," to quote Bunyan's Greatheart, is a "most dangerous place" for heaven-bound pilgrims. "For if at any time the pilgrims meet with any brunt, it is when they forget what favours they have received, and how unworthy they are of them."

The story of the Free Church of Scotland is indeed a record of Divine favour toward a people who, more than once, risked their all for Christ's sake. We tell it again with the prayer that it may serve to strengthen the loyalty of Free Church people everywhere to the Church of their fathers, and stimulate them to share with others, in every way possible, the teaching of our Scottish Reformers to which the Free Church of Scotland is pledged by her unequivocal acceptance of the Westminster Confession of Faith as her principal subordinate standard. It is the Faith there formulated that sustained the Scottish Church under the many fiery trials of her long history, and that will, we believe, be the means in God's hand of reviving the soul of Scotland in the better days for which, in dependence upon His promise, we look.

G. N. M. Collins.

CONTENTS

CHAPTER ONE

THE CHURCH MAKES A NEW BEGINNING

**It is not a new and strange ensign which I have
unfurled, but Thy noble standard, O Lord.**—*John
Knox.*

The General Assembly of the Church of Scotland which
convened in Edinburgh on 18th May 1843 opened in highly
unusual circumstances. It was a day of general excitement;
Thomas Brown tells us all about it in his *Annals of the
Disruption.* Crowds had been gathering around the doors of St
Andrew's Church, George Street, where the Assembly was to be
held, since day-break. And, about a mile away, in the Canonmills
district of the city the large Tanfield Hall had been prepared to
house a second Assembly, and the streets connecting the two
buildings were lined with people who were waiting to see the
procession of churchmen who were expected, later in the day, to
make their way from the old place of assembly to the new.

Following the customary service in the High Kirk, Professor
David Welsh, D.D., who had preached the sermon there,
proceeded to St Andrew's Church where, as Moderator of the
preceding General Assembly, he would normally have constituted
the Assembly of 1843. But when he arose to speak, it was not to
offer the usual prayer of constitution, but, after a brief prayer for
blessing, to explain that the Assembly could not proceed with its
business "without a violation of the terms of the Union between
Church and State in this land, as now authoritatively declared".
Thereupon he read the Church's *Protest,* setting forth the reasons
why she could no longer submit to the encroachments of the civil
courts upon her rightful province as guaranteed, not only by
successive enactments of her own supreme Court, but also by the
legislation of the State itself.

The *Protest* made it clear that those whose views it expressed
had no quarrel with the Establishment Principle itself; their
grievance was that this Principle was now being used perversely to
justify the repeated intrusions which the State had made, of
recent years, into the field of ecclesiastical jurisdiction;
furthermore, that the representations made by the aggrieved
Church had been set aside. "We are not responsible," they say in
the closing words of the *Protest,* "for any consequences that may
follow from this our enforced separation from an Establishment
which we loved and prized."[1]

1

Having read the *Protest*, Dr Welsh laid the document upon the table and bowed respectfully to the Queen's Commissioner in token of continued loyalty to the Throne, notwithstanding that the State, by recent legislation, had set the seal of its approval upon the actions of the civil courts in depriving the Church of her spiritual independence. He thereupon left the building, accompanied by some of the most distinguished ministers in the Church and followed by a great company of ministers and elders who were of one mind with them. To the acclamations of the crowds in the streets they made their way to the Tanfield Hall.

Arrived there, Dr Welsh took the chair without any motion being proposed that he should do so. His action, as Professor G. D. Henderson puts it, "involved a claim, often repeated, that the gathering was still the Assembly of the Church of Scotland, though now free from the State connection, that in fact the Disruption was that of the Church from the State."[2] And there the Retiring Moderator of the previous Assembly did what he normally would have done in St Andrew's Church; he constituted the General Assembly, and the Church of Scotland Free began its business. Having held firmly and unambiguously to the historic constitution of Scotland's national Church as agreed at the Revolution Settlement of 1690, and guaranteed by the Act of Union of the English and Scottish Parliaments in 1707, these men rightly believed that their entitlement to be known as the true Church of Scotland was unassailable; and they said so. For the very first Act which they passed in the Tanfield Hall Assembly contains this paragraph: "And we farther protest, that any Assembly constituted in submission to the conditions now declared to be law, and under the civil coercion which has been brought to bear in the election of Commissioners to the Assembly this day appointed to have been holden, and on the Commissioners chosen thereto, is not, and shall not be deemed, a lawful and free Assembly of the Church of Scotland, according to the original and fundamental principles thereof . . . ."[3]

Lord Macaulay, in a reference to the ecclesiastical events of 1843, has no hesitation in lending his support to this claim. "Suppose," he says, "that we could call up from their graves the Presbyterian divines who sat in the General Assembly when the compact between England and Scotland was made; suppose that we could call up Carstares; that we could call up Boston, the author of *The Fourfold State*; that we could relate to them the history of the ecclesiastical revolutions which have, since their time, taken place in Scotland; and that we could ask them, 'Is the Established Church, or is the Free Church, identical with the Church which existed at the time of the Union?' Is it not quite certain what their answer would be? They would say . . . 'Our

2

Church was the Church of Chalmers and Brewster, not the Church of Bryce and Mair'."[4]

The nomination of Dr Thomas Chalmers as Moderator in succession to Dr Welsh was enthusiastically carried, for his gifts of leadership had already been fully proved. As the spokesman of the Fathers and Brethren who had broken with the Establishment, he carried them with him in the exposition of the Church's claim which he gave in his Moderatorial address.

"We hold," he said, "that every part and every function of a commonwealth should be leavened with Christianity, and that every functionary, from the highest to the lowest, should in their respective spheres do all that in them lies to countenance and uphold it. That is to say, though we quit the Establishment, we go out on the Establishment Principle* — we quit a vitiated Establishment, but would rejoice in returning to a pure one. To express it otherwise, we are advocates for a national recognition and national support of religion, and we are not Voluntaries."[5]

The Deed of Demission which the ministerial members of Assembly subsequently signed expressed their determination to maintain their ecclesiastical heritage, abandoning nothing except the material benefits which went with State endowment.

The following extract from the Deed is worth quoting.

"And farther, the said ministers and elders, in this their General Assembly convened, while they refuse to acknowledge the supreme ecclesiastical judicatory established by law in Scotland, and now holding its sittings in Edinburgh, to be a free Assembly of the Church of Scotland, or a lawful Assembly of the said Church, according to the true and original constitution thereof, and disclaim its authority as to matters spiritual, yet in respect of

*In discussing spiritual independence reference has to be made to Erastianism, Voluntaryism, and the Establishment Principle. Brief definitions are therefore necessary.

Erastianism takes its name from Thomas Erastus, who became Professor of Medicine at Heidelberg in 1558. Erastus had also studied theology, and took a special interest in ecclesiastical discipline. After his death his views in this connection were developed beyond the limits which he had observed until, in its full-blown form, Erastianism came to represent the Church merely as a department of the State.

The Establishment Principle, on the other hand, stresses that the Church has a special government of its own into which the civil ruler may not intrude. Church and State are the twin departments of Christ's Kingdom on earth, each owing duty and service to the other, and both being concerned with the prerogatives of Christ as Head of the Church and King of the kings of the earth. The aim of both should be the production and maintenance of a Christian civilisation. It is the Church's duty to instruct the State in righteousness, and, reciprocally, the State is duty bound to support national religion, although not by coercive measures. Such "establishment" does not necessarily include endowment, although support of national religion in this way would have the effect of extending the benefits of the Church's ministry even to the poorest regions of the country.

Voluntaryism is the flat contradiction of Establishment. Professor James Bannerman gives as the fundamental maxim of the Voluntary theory of Church and State that "the State, as the State, has nothing to do with religion." Dr James Begg pinpoints the fundamental error of Voluntaryism where he says, "It confounds the State with the world, forgetting that civil government is a Divine ordinance, and that the magistrate is a minister of God unto the people for good."

3

the recognition given to it by the State, and the powers, in consequence of such recognition, belonging to it, with reference to the temporalities of the Establishment, and the rights derived thereto from the State, hereby appoint a duplicate of this Act to be subscribed by their Moderator, and also by the several ministers, members of this Assembly, now present in Edinburgh, for their individual interests, to be transmitted to the clerk of the said ecclesiastical judicatory by law established, for the purpose of certiorating them that the benefices held by such of the said ministers, or others adhering to this Assembly, as were incumbents of benefices, are now vacant; and the said parties consent that the said benefices shall be dealt with as such."[6]

In claiming spiritual independence for the Church, the Disruption Fathers—as those first ministers of the Free Church of Scotland are commonly called—were at pains to show that they were making no new demand, but merely reiterating a claim which had been made, and upheld, time and again, ever since the Scottish Reformation three centuries before. Indeed, as Chalmers pointed out, even anterior to her connection with the State, "the Church had a government of her own, acting in her own proper sphere, with certain inherent liberties which, save by reason of persecution, were not violated." When she entered into connection with the State "she gave up no part of her liberties; it was her inalienable birthright, with which she would not part."[7]

The plan of a Christian nation had been before the Scottish Reformers from the beginning and, at the request of Parliament, they had drawn up their *Scots Confession* in 1560. This credal statement, by Parliamentary acceptance, became the national Confession. Its Protestant doctrine was ratified, and the Church was established. Not until 1567, however, was the Church endowed. This is a fact of weighty significance; for it shows that the Church's claim to spiritual independence was recognised from the very beginning of her existence as an Established Church, and that establishment and endowment are not inseparable privileges. The Church carried her spiritual freedom into establishment in 1560, and she sacrificed no part of it when she became an endowed establishment in 1567. When therefore the claim to spiritual independence was made by the Disruption Fathers, they were at pains to show that it was not new.

Verification of this claim is to be found in the *First Book of Discipline*, another foundation document of the Church, produced in 1560. There the principle of democratic ecclesiastical government is clearly set forth in the phrase, "It appertaineth to the people, and to every several congregation, to elect their minister." When, through negligence, the congregation failed to exercise this right within a reasonable time, an alternative way of effecting a ministerial settlement might be allowed; but even then the concurrence of the people in the choice of pastor was to be sought, for it was distinctly specified as a thing "altogether . . . to be avoided, that any man be violently intruded or thrust in upon, any congregation."

The submission of the *First Book of Discipline* had the effect of revealing that the enthusiasm of some of the Scottish nobles for the Reformation was not as sincere as it seemed. The reformation of the Church was needed; that they would all have agreed. But when it became evident that the Reformers planned to reclaim certain Church lands and properties which, by one means or another, had passed into the hands of the nobility, and apply this church patrimony to religious, educational and social purposes the reforming zeal of the nobles concerned lost much of its ardour. Furthermore, the return of the young Queen, Mary, from France in 1561, and the setting up of her Court in Edinburgh, was a strong inducement to seek favour in royal circles. But the policies of the queen and those of Knox were so completely contrary to each other that to try to hold in with both sides became not less difficult than to serve God and Mammon. William Maitland of Lethington was one of those who found it so. Maitland was one of the ablest Scottish statesmen of his time. Mary's choice of him was a master-stroke of diplomacy. Maitland was known to be a Protestant, and his appointment as the Queen's Secretary would appear to augur well for the Queen's Protestant subjects, and for the future of Protestantism in the country. And since one good turn deserves another, Maitland, and other Protestant leaders similarly favoured, would regard themselves as bound to safeguard the interests of the Crown against the uncompromising Knox who was proof alike against bribery and brow-beating. "Others", they said, "sned* the branches of the Papistry; he strikes at the root."[8]

In these circumstances it was inevitable that tensions should develop.

Within a few months of Mary's return to Scotland, Maitland expressed doubt as to the legality of General Assemblies of the Church held without the Queen's authority. But Knox was unyielding. "Take from us the freedom of Assemblies," he said, "and take from us the evangel; for without Assemblies how shall good order and unity in doctrine be kept?"[9]

Knox was well aware that Mary's dislike of Assemblies arose from her determination to establish her own arbitrary authority, and to restore Popery. "You have taught the people," she charged, "to receive another religion than their princes can allow, and how can that doctrine be of God, seeing that God commands subjects to obey their princes?"

* Lopped.

5

"Madam," replied Knox, "as right religion took neither original strength nor authority from worldly princes, but from the eternal God alone, so are not subjects bound to frame their religion according to the appetite of their princes."

At this point Mary's diplomacy failed her. "I will defend the Kirk of Rome," she stormed, "for I think it is the true Kirk of God."

But the stubborn Reformer who "neither feared nor flattered flesh," stood his ground. "Your will, Madam," he replied, "is no reason; neither doth your thought make that Roman harlot to be the true and immaculate spouse of Jesus Christ."[10]

The quick-witted and strong-willed young Queen, who had ascended her Scottish throne with the avowed intention of restoring good relations between Scotland and France, and of reclaiming the Scottish Church for the Roman obedience, met her match in the one-time galley slave who, in the inscrutable providence of God, had been raised up and equipped by hard experience to become the champion of the Church's independence in his native Scotland. His reply to Maitland, linking the freedom of Assemblies with the maintenance of the Evangel was not the retort of an obstinate bigot but the shrewd judgment of a far-seeing statesman and prophet.

In making her stand for spiritual freedom, the Church (and this has to be said with emphasis) kept well within the limits of her own charter. The pre-Reformation Church had frequently transgressed her proper bounds and encroached upon the province of the State; but the Reformed Church contended only for the rights and liberties that had been guaranteed to her in her contract with the State. She made no claim to be above civil law in the ordinary affairs of life. But in such matters as fell within recognised ecclesiastical jurisdiction—the appointing of office-bearers, the exercise of discipline, the formulation of the Church's constitution and Confession, the conduct of public worship and the administration of the sacraments—in these she claimed an autonomy that was clearly deducible from the teaching of Holy Scripture. The maintenance and defence of these inalienable rights constituted a sacred trust which had been committed to her by Christ Himself.

1. *Free Church Assembly Proceedings*, May 1843; pp. 6, 7.
2. G. D. Henderson, *Heritage;* p. 109.
3. *Free Church Assembly Proceedings*, May 1843; p. 7.
4. D. A. Mackinnon, *Some Chapters in Scottish Church History;* p. 196.
5. *Free Church Assembly Proceedings*, May 1843; p. 12.
6. See *Deed of Demission*, in *Authorised Standards of the Free Church.*
7. *Free Church Assembly Proceedings*, May 1843; p. 12.
8. Croft Dickenson, *Knox's History of the Reformation;* p. xxxiii.
9. ibid., p. lx.
10. T. McCrie, *Life of John Knox;* 1855 edn.; p. 180.

CHAPTER TWO

THE TWO KINGDOMS

Christ lives and reigns alone in His Church, and will have all done therein according to His Word and will . . . He has given no supreme Headship over His Church to any Pope, King, or Parliament whatsoever . . .—*Johnston of Warriston.*

The opposition to the Church's doctrine of spiritual independence had its source, not in religious scruple, but in the lust for temporal advancement and material gain.

It has to be remembered that the pre-Reformation Church in Scotland had become enormously wealthy. Everything in the service of the Church had its price, and the price was unsparingly claimed. "Nae penny, nae Paternoster," became a common saying among the people. "Purgatory," writes Dr Hay Fleming, "occupied the foremost place among remunerative inventions. By it, the clergy preyed not only on the fears of the dying, but on the affection and the remorse of the relatives of the dead." Corpse-presents and mortuary dues were so exorbitantly rated and ruthlessly exacted as to become a public scandal. Vast legacies of land and money were left to the Church in the superstitious hope that these would somehow be set to the credit of the testators in another world. In a letter of Cardinal Sermoneta to the Pope in 1556 it was acknowledged that "almost one half of the revenue of the whole kingdom of Scotland" had found its way into the coffers of the Church.

The rejection of the Roman Catholic Church by the Scottish people and Parliament in 1560 raised questions as to the disposal of this vast wealth. Knox and his fellow-Reformers made their proposals in the *First Book of Discipline.* They were as follows:

1. The rents of the Church lands which belonged to the bishoprics ought to go to the maintenance of the Universities, and to the Church's superintendents who had been given special, and temporary, duties of administration and oversight until the ministry of the Church should be more adequately reconstituted.

2. The teinds, which for so long had gone to the support of the clergy, were to be retained and used for the support of the local ministers and schoolmasters (for the Reformers planned to have not only a church but also a school in every parish), and for the relief of the poor.

3. The rents and annual subsidies which used to be paid to

all persons. The General Assembly was forbidden to meet without his permission, and the effective jurisdiction of the Church was lodged in the Episcopal body. Once again, and in no uncertain way, the supremacy of the Crown was being asserted in the Church as well as in the State.

But James was adept at trimming his sails to suit the breeze. Sensing his dependence upon Presbyterian support he called a meeting of the Assembly in 1586 and showed his readiness to come to terms with his Presbyterian subjects. The Black Acts were repealed in 1590. The king declared his favour for the Reformed Kirk which he now praised as "the sincerest Kirk in the world." But if sincerity was a quality in the Church it certainly was lacking in the king, for James was soon re-asserting his supremacy in all her affairs.

The immediate cause of conflict on this occasion was a plot to overthrow the Protestant religion in Scotland. The principal agents of this conspiracy were the Earls of Huntly, Angus and Errol. Their plans came to light in 1592, but the scheming nobles were treated with such leniency by the king as to give rise to the suspicion that he himself had papist leanings.

Again, Andrew Melville headed a deputation sent by a meeting of ministers at Cupar to remonstrate with the king. But James was "crabbed and choleric" and not in a mood to hear such representations. Wrathfully, he counter-charged the Church with sedition and rebuked the ministers for meeting without his permission.

It was then that Melville made his famous remonstrance. Plucking the king's sleeve, and describing him as God's "sillie vassal" (or feeble servant) he reminded him of the protestations which the Church had already made to him in defence of her proper freedom. "Sir," he proceeded, "we will always reverence your majesty in public; but since we have this occasion to be with your Majesty in private, and since you are brought into extreme danger both of your life and crown, and along with you, the country and the Church of God are like to go to wreck for not telling you the truth and giving you faithful counsel, we must discharge our duty, or else be traitors both to Christ and you. Therefore, Sir, as divers times before I have told you, so now again I must tell you, there are two kings and two kingdoms in Scotland; there is King James, the head of this Commonwealth, and there is King Jesus the King of the Church, whose subject King James the Sixth is, and of whose Kingdom he is not a king, nor a lord, nor a head, but a member. We will yield to you your place, and give you all due obedience; but again I say, you are not the head of the Church. . . ."

Realising that threats and insults were wasted on the dauntless commissioner, James changed his tone and sent the deputation away with fair promises which he had no intention of honouring. For James was the supreme example of royal attitudinarianism. An absolutist to the core, he never once lost sight of his objective, and if at any time he appeared to be in concessive mood towards the Church it was only because he judged that mood to be best suited to his interests in the circumstances of the hour.

His next move was made with characteristic astuteness. Pretending to be at a disadvantage in the outworking of his ecclesiastical policy, because he had no authoritative ecclesiastical council with whom to consult when matters of difficulty arose, he requested the General Assembly to appoint a commission that would meet this need. The request seemed reasonable, and in meeting it the Assembly judged that they were taking steps towards the establishment of a proper relationship between the Church and the Crown. But no sooner had the ecclesiastical commissioners been appointed than the king declared them to constitute the Third Estate in the realm, and, accordingly, invited the Church's representatives to take their place in Parliament with the rank of bishops. This distasteful designation, he hastened to assure them, was to be regarded as purely titular. "I wish not," he explained, "to bring in papistical or Anglican bishops, but only to have the best and wisest of the ministry appointed by the General Assembly to have place in Council and Parliament, to sit upon their own matters and see them done, and not to stand always at the door like poor supplicants, despised and nothing regarded."

What could be fairer than that? The Episcopalian title was to be used merely as a convenience in order to obtain privileges for the Presbyterian Church! Just as in the case of the "Tulchan" bishops! But some of the older members of the Assembly were becoming used to the king's tergiversation, and they remained unconvinced by his promises of fair dealing. Shrewd David Fergusson of Dunfermline compared the king's plan for the introduction of his titular bishops into the ministry of the Scottish Church to the wooden horse device whereby the Greeks captured Troy. James Melville, the like-minded nephew of the intrepid Andrew, spoke of it as "the needle which drew in the episcopal thread," and John Davidson of Prestonpans made it clear that he was not deceived by the king's strategy. "Ay," said he, "busk, busk, busk him as bonnilie as ye can, and fetch him in as fairly as ye will; we see him weill eneuch, we see the horns of his mitre."

The menace of the "horns of the mitre" soon became more evident once James succeeded to the English throne. At last, he declared, he had "reached the promised land where religion was

11

professed in its purity," and where he sat "among grave, learned and reverent men" and was not "as formerly, a king without a State and honour, nor in a place where order was banished and beardless boys would brave him to his face."

With strengthened hand, James now proceeded to make his royal power more fully felt in his northern realm. He suppressed the right of holding free Assemblies of the Scottish Church, and when a few ministers, in defiance of his ban, dared to meet as an Assembly in Aberdeen in 1605 the king's reaction was to imprison some and banish others. The charge, of course, was disloyalty and treason; but John Welsh, Knox's son-in-law, who was one of those upon whom the king's displeasure fell, wrote from his prison-cell at Blackness a truer assessment of the situation. "These two points," he declared, "first, that Christ is the Head of the Church; secondly, that she is free in her government from all other jurisdiction except Christ's . . . are the special cause of our imprisonment, being now convicted as traitors for the maintaining thereof."

The anglicisation of the Scottish Church continued, and two General Assemblies of the Church were particularly noteworthy in this process.

The first of these gatherings was held in Glasgow in 1610 and was derisively described as the "angelical" Assembly. But the "angels" present were not heavenly bodies but merely golden coins called angels which, on the direction of the king's commissioner were distributed among the ministers to purchase their suffrages for the king's plans. Royal missives had already been sent to the presbyteries of the Church indicating the persons who should be sent to the Assembly as their representatives. An attempt was made to give a semblance of respectability to the bribery practised at the Assembly by representing that the money distributed to members was merely to help with the expenses of the poorer ministers and of those who had come long distances. But John Row exposes this shameful pretence by showing that some of the recipients of the "angels" lived in or near Glasgow, where the Assembly was held, and "some gracious ministers in the north', who voted negative, got no gold at all."

By this travesty of ecclesiastical procedure James succeeded in his plan of taking the calling of General Assemblies into his own prerogative, and of securing recognition of the bishops as moderators of the diocesan synods.

The second of the Assemblies referred to as having been convened for the purpose of advancing episcopacy in Scotland was held at Perth in 1618. Again, it was a "packed" Assembly, and the legislation known as the Five Articles of Perth had an easy passage. By these Articles it was ordained (1) that the Lord's

12

Supper should be received kneeling; (2) that it might be administered in private; (3) that Baptism also might be in private; (4) that children should be confirmed; and (5) that Christmas, Good Friday, Easter, Ascension and Pentecost should be observed as holidays.[6]

For a time the passing of these Acts had very little effect. The bishops still lacked the power to enforce them, and the king was well aware that any attempt at coercion would spread disaffection among his Scottish subjects and unsettle his throne. It was one thing to have his way in packed and bribed Assemblies; it was quite another to win the support of the masses of the people.

James was prepared to bide his time, but it was slow to come. When he died in 1625 the Scottish people were still strongly Presbyterian. The new king had less kingcraft than his father, and his accession boded ill both for Scotland and for its royal house.

1. Hay Fleming, *The Reformation in Scotland;* p. 525.
2. J. H. Burton, *History of Scotland;* vol. 5, pp. 81, 82.
3. T. McCrie, *Life of Andrew Melville;* p. 85.
4. ibid. 181.
5. R. M. Gillon, *John Davidson of Prestonpans;* p. 175.
6. J. Macpherson, *History of the Church in Scotland;* p. 172.

CHAPTER THREE

THE NATIONAL COVENANT

Persecution for conscience sake, and oppression in civil liberty, flow from the same spring, are carried on by the same measures, and lead to the same miserable end.—*Robert Woodrow.*

Towards the end of his long reign, King James VI had much reason to feel pleased with the outworking of his policy regarding the Scottish Church. His measures against the Presbyterian leaders, and his favourable treatment of the bishops, had made him master of the situation. He had got rid of Andrew Melville by, first of all, excluding him from the General Assemblies, then by summoning him to London where, on a paltry charge, he imprisoned him in the Tower for four years, finally permitting him to retire to France, where he served as Professor at Sedan for the remainder of his life. Episcopacy fitted in well with the absolutism of the king, and by the time of his death in 1625, fostered by royal patronage, the bishops had acquired great authority in Scotland, and it was reckoned that at least half of the civil offices in the country were occupied by these favoured churchmen. But although Episcopacy became the recognised Church order, it still had little favour among the masses of the people, as events soon proved.

Charles I came to the throne even more obsessed with belief in the Divine Right of Kings than his father had been; and this meant that his antipathy to Presbyterianism was correspondingly greater. The sovereign must be supreme in all causes; the subject's one duty was to obey.

The king's evil genius in Church affairs was William Laud, an ambitious pluralist who, by preferment after preferment, reached the primacy of the English Church in 1633. A rabid anti-Puritan since student days, Laud made it his great aim to root out Calvinism in England and Presbyterianism in Scotland. The caution of King James may have served to curb his zeal in this connection, but Charles was a monarch after his own heart. Neither man was amenable to the counsel of prudence. The Earl of Loudoun had warned Charles on the occasion of his first visit to Scotland after his accession, "Sire, the people of Scotland will obey you in everything with the utmost cheerfulness, provided you do not touch their religion and conscience." But Charles was intractable. And as for Laud, Robert Baillie declares, "He would break ere he bow one inch; he is born it seems for his own and our destruction; yet there is a God."

Scotland has little cause to remember either Charles or his Archbishop with gratitude.

The Five Articles of Perth, introducing Episcopalian practices, although passed in the reign of James, were not strictly enforced until Charles came to the throne. Resentment however was building up, and it reached flashpoint in 1637 when Charles commanded that Laud's Liturgy should be used throughout Scotland. The story of the riot in the High Kirk of Edinburgh, on the 23rd day of July 1637, is too well known to require repetition here. Whatever part Jenny Geddes and her stool played in the ecclesiastical events of that day, the attempt of Dean Hannay to introduce Laud's Liturgy led to a general rising that the king and his advisers could never have foreseen. Scotland had had enough! The Church's claim to spiritual independence, so often presented, so often granted, and yet so often violated, was once more to be submitted—this time with a determination that ruthless persecution and oppression would not be able to break.

"Wha's fule now?" asked Archie Armstrong the king's jester, on meeting Archbishop Laud after the news from Edinburgh had reached London. Laud's chagrin can be judged from the fact that, at his instigation, Armstrong was brought before the Privy Council, deprived of his fool's coat and dismissed from the king's service. But Archie had the last word. When someone asked him afterwards what had become of his coat of office, he replied, "O, my lord of Canterbury hath taken it from me, because he or some of the Scotch bishops may have need of it themselves; but he hath given me a black coat for it to cover my knavery withal."[1]

Knowing that Charles would never consent to their demand for spiritual liberty the Scottish people now organised their defence. Within a few months a large committee was set up, representing the nobility, the gentry, the clergy and the burgesses. The committee was known as The Tables, and it fell into the four representative sections indicated.

It was at this juncture that Alexander Henderson came into prominence. Henderson was undoubtedly the man for the hour. Formerly a prelatist himself he had been appointed to the parish of Leuchars—very much against the wishes of the parishioners, who had gone the length of barricading the doors of the church against him on the day set for his induction, thereby making it necessary for him and the officiating clergy to enter the building by a window. Soon thereafter Robert Bruce of Kinnaird, the famous Presbyterian divine who had been expelled from the charge of the High Kirk of Edinburgh because of his opposition to King James's arbitrary intrusion into ecclesiastical affairs, was

15

preaching in the neighbourhood of Leuchars, and the young minister of that parish went to hear him, muffling himself up well and stealing quietly into a dark corner of the building lest he should be recognised. But when the preacher gave out his text, *"Verily, verily, I say unto you, he that entereth not by the door into the sheep-fold, but climbeth up some other way, the same is a thief and a robber,"* Henderson regarded it as a personal message from One Whose eye pierces through every pretence and penetrates to every dark corner.[2]

From the time of his conversion, Henderson cast in his lot with the Presbyterian party in the Church. His preaching found a new key-note, and the people who had been so bitterly opposed to him at his first coming among them now became his devoted followers. His appointment to Leuchars had been his reward from the Episcopalian party for his zeal in opposing the influence of Andrew Melville at St Andrews; now, by a divine irony, the cloak of Melville descended upon him, and, for the rest of his life, he preached the faith which once he had laboured to destroy.

This was the man who, under God, guided the Scottish Church through her Second Reformation.

The decision to organise the struggle for independence under a National Covenant had the effect of linking the movement with an earlier national bond which had been drawn up on the instruction of King James VI in 1581. It was a time when spiritual loyalties were fickle and uncertain, and Jesuit activity was widespread. The king himself was not above suspicion, for he was known to be much under the influence of his kinsman Esmé Stewart, and Stewart was regarded as an emissary of the Papal house of Guise, sent across from France for the sole purpose of winning over the young king to the Roman obedience. To remove suspicion from himself therefore, and to secure the loyal support of his Protestant subjects, James had instructed John Craig, his chaplain, to draw up the *King's Confession,* in which the signatories, abjuring the errors of the Church of Rome and professing loyalty to Protestantism, bound themselves "that we shall continue in the obedience of the doctrine and discipline of this kirk, and shall defend the same, according to our vocation and power, all the days of our lives; under the pains contained in the law, and danger both of body and soul in the days of God's fearful judgment."[3]

This Confession, signed in the first instance by the king and his household, was afterwards, by an order in Council and an Act of General Assembly, subscribed by all ranks of the people throughout the country.

In making the *King's Confession* the basis of the *National Covenant* of 1638 the Covenanters were safeguarding themselves from a charge of rebellious conduct. They were merely renewing a solemn bond, proposed by the king and gladly accepted by his subjects, that they would uphold the civil and spiritual liberties granted under the Reformation settlement. The pledge of loyalty to the king's person and throne, given in the earlier Confession, was renewed in 1638. The earlier document, naturally, had to be expanded and brought up to date. This work fell into two main parts. The first of these, which was a statement of the Acts of Parliament by which the Presbyterian Church had been established in Scotland, was entrusted to Archibald Johnston of Warriston; and the second, setting forth the terms of the covenant to be entered into, was assigned to Alexander Henderson. The errors and innovations brought into the Church under the rule of the bishops were repudiated and rejected, and the vow was solemnly taken that we shall "resist these contrary errors and corruptions, according to our vocation, and to the utmost of that power that God hath put in our hands, all the days of our life; and in like manner with the same heart, we declare before GOD and Men, That we have no intention nor desire to attempt anything that may turne to the dishonour of GOD, or to the diminution of the King's greatness and authority: But on the contrary, we promise and sweare, that we shall, to the uttermost of our power, with our meanes and lives, stand to the defence of our dread Soveraigne, the King's Majesty, his Person and Authority, in the defence and preservation of the foresaid true Religion, Liberties and Lawes of the Kingdome: as also to the mutual defence and assistance, every one of us of another in the same cause of maintaining the true Religion and His Majesty's authority, with our best counsel, our bodies, meanes, and whole power, against all sorts of persons whatsoever. . . ."[4]

The need for personal piety is recognised by the signatories, for they conclude, "And because we cannot look for a blessing from God upon our proceedings, except with our Profession and Subscription we join such a life and conversation as beseemeth Christians, who have renewed their covenant with God; We, therefore, faithfully promise, for ourselves, our followers, and all other under us, both in publick, in our particular families, and personal carriage, to endeavour to keep ourselves within the bounds of Christian liberty, and to be good examples to others of all Godlinesse, Sobernesse, and Righteousnesse, and of every duety we owe to God and Man. . . ."[5]

That the country was ready for such a manifesto as the Covenant provided was evident from the bounding enthusiasm with which it was received. To the more percipient of the prelatic party the portents were plain. "We have been making a tub these

17

forty years," ruefully exclaimed Archbishop Spottiswoode of St Andrews, "and now the bottom thereof is fallen out."

The deep feeling, yet sober wording, of the *National Covenant* was matched by the spirit of reverent determination which prevailed at the signing of it. This was no common uprising instigated by an inflamed and reckless mob, as events proved. The conscience of the people had been touched. Their God-given liberties were being infringed. Their Church was being made a mere department of State. The laws of Christ's Kingdom were being over-written by the civil authorities. Setting aside the Word of God and the rights of a Christian people the State had set up its own form of ecclesiastical government in which the king was supreme. And as if that were not enough, it was now prescribing the form of the people's worship and the content of their faith in a Liturgy which Principal Hugh Watt aptly describes as "Canterbury amended by Rome."[6]

The *National Covenant* of 1638 was the authentic voice of Reformed Scotland.

The famous Covenanting Assembly which met in Glasgow Cathedral in November 1638 was a thoroughly representative gathering. Its 240 members included several of the ablest men in the ministry of the Church at the time, and of its ruling elders seventeen were high-ranking nobles, nine were Knights, twenty-five were Barons entitled to sit in Parliament, and forty-seven were Burgesses. Its mood was resolute; its decisions far-reaching. With Alexander Henderson in the Moderatorial Chair, the Assembly asserted its authority as a government "distinct from civil government" which Christ Himself had instituted in His Church. The Five Articles of Perth, that troublesome legacy from the reign of James VI, were annulled; the Book of Canons and Laud's Liturgy were rejected; the bishops were removed from office; the whole fabric of Episcopacy was overthrown.

In his choice of Commissioner, King Charles could hardly have been more misguided. Of royal Stewart blood himself, the Marquis of Hamilton shared the prejudices of the king and let the fact be known. In a letter to Charles he declared that "next to hell, he hated Scotland."[7] The Glasgow Assembly he described as, "for the most part totallie voyd of learning"—a statement that required no more for its refutation than just the bare mention of the illustrious names that appeared on the roll of the Assembly. David Masson, a more competent critic, was nearer the mark when he wrote, "The first properly historical Covenanters" were "simply the whole flower and strength of the Scottish Nation from the highest peerage to the lowest peasantry."[8]

In such a gathering, Hamilton's remonstrances were utterly without avail. In vain did he call upon the Moderator to close the

Assembly with prayer; and when he voiced his objections to the decisions taken, and endeavoured to nullify these by dissolving the Assembly, the commissioners refused to recognise his, or the King's authority in such a matter. "Albeit we have acknowledged the power of Christian kings for the convening of Assemblies," said the Moderator, "yet that we may not derogate from Christ's right; for He hath given Divine warrants to convocate assemblies, whether magistrates consent or not."

In gracious terms he paid tribute to the royal Commissioner's zeal in executing the commands of his sovereign and found therein a reminder to the Assembly to be not less zealous toward *their* Lord, and to maintain the rights and privileges of His Kingdom. And when the King's representative and a few ministers retired from the Assembly the remaining members signified their wholehearted adherence to a protestation, prepared in anticipation by Lord Rothes, and read by the Clerk in the following terms: "In the name of the Lord Jesus Christ, the only Head and monarch of His Church, from a consciousness of our duty to God and His truth, this kingdom, this Assembly, and her freedom, we profess, with heavy and loyal hearts, we cannot dissolve this Assembly."[9]

Nor did they until their work was done. Once again it was enacted that "no person shall be intruded in any office of the Church contrary to the will of the congregation to which they are appointed". The democratic spirit of Scottish Presbyterianism again asserted itself, and the Church rejoiced in her regained freedom. "We have now cast down the walls of Jericho," declared Alexander Henderson when, after sitting for a month, the Assembly had completed its work; "let him that rebuildeth them beware of the curse of Hiel the Bethelite."[10]

Dr J. King Hewison succinctly summarises the results of the Glasgow Assembly of 1638 as follows: "The Word of God, as the sole rule of faith and morals, was restored to its authoritative position; the Lord Jesus Christ was again enthroned as the Head of the Church; the principle of autocracy was condemned; the seat of power was asserted to be in the people, as taught by Buchanan, Goodman, and other Reformers; the national will regarding religion expressed in the Covenant was unmistakably announced; Episcopacy, as a barren and unwelcome imposition, was extinguished; Scottish Presbytery, as a polity warranted by Scripture, was revived; the right of the laity to representation in the Church Courts was ratified; and the personal interests of individuals in their own spiritual welfare was so quickened, that, for long after 1638, the printing presses of Scotland poured out a flood of books and pamphlets, indicating the joy and satisfaction which the emancipation of the Church had conferred."[11]

That Assembly has sometimes been criticised for, as it is alleged, exceeding its rightful powers and setting aside Acts of Parliament relating to the establishment of Episcopacy as the order of the Scottish Church. But the fact that must not be overlooked is that the State had gone beyond its proper province in passing those Acts, and that what the Glasgow Assembly of 1638 did was to resist and nullify legislation that was unconstitutional for the civil power to enact. They were well aware that the consequences of their resistance would be grave. "The wind is now on Christ's face in this land," wrote Samuel Rutherford to Henderson, "and seeing ye are with Him ye cannot expect the leeside or the sunny side of the brae."[12]

For the breaking of the storm they did not have long to wait.

1. A. Cameron, *The Church of our Fathers*; p. 126.
2. ibid. pp. 129, 130.
3. J. D. Douglas, *Light in the North*; p. 198.
4. ibid p. 204.
5. ibid. p. 205.
6. H. Watt, *The Scottish Covenants*; p. 11.
7. J. King Hewison, *The Covenanters*, vol. 1; p. 284.
8. ibid. pp. 298, 299.
9. T. McCrie, *Sketches of Church History*, vol 1; p. 231.
10. ibid. p. 237.
11. J. King Hewison, *The Covenanters*, vol. 1; p. 316.
12. S. Rutherford, *Letters*; 115.

CHAPTER FOUR

KIRK AND CROWN IN CONFLICT

Ye that are the people of God do not weary to maintain the testimony of the day in your stations and places, and whatsoever ye do, make sure of an interest in Christ, for there is a storm coming that shall try your foundation.—*James Renwick.*

The king's immediate reaction to the Church's rejection of Episcopacy was to embark on military preparations for the invasion of Scotland. "I will rather die," he told the Marquis of Hamilton — "than yield to those impertinent and damnable demands."[1] Fawning sycophants assured him that a show of military strength would be sufficient to change the mood of his northern subjects. But the miscalculations of the king and his counsellors were disastrous in their consequences. The Covenanters had anticipated his action and were ready for the confrontation. A Scottish army numbering some 30,000 men under the command of General Alexander Leslie (afterwards Earl of Leven)—one of the best military strategists of his day—took up a commanding position at Dunse Law against the king's forces. The lettering on the Scottish colours FOR CHRIST'S CROWN AND COVENANT, proclaimed the sacred cause which had brought them together. Alexander Henderson was with them as a chaplain, and so too, in a similar capacity, were George Gillespie, John Livingstone, Robert Baillie, and several like-minded ministerial brethren from the country parishes.

The Scottish leaders were at pains to remove any misapprehensions that their neighbours south of the Border might have formed concerning their intentions. They were, they said, "coming amongst them as their friends.' They would not despoil them of anything, "from a thread even to a shoe latchet." They had not forgotten the help of their English friends in their struggle against France, and their desire was "to link the two nations together in straiter and stronger bonds, both of civil and Christian love, than ever before."

The advantage, in every way, lay with the Scots. They were banded together in a worthy cause which commanded the deepest loyalty of their hearts. Their leader, and several of his subordinate officers, had served in the wars of Gustavus Adolphus, the saviour of Protestantism in the Thirty Years' War in Germany. The nation was behind them, and their hearts were strong in the conviction that their cause was just. Charles was less fortunate. The morale of his army was poor, and it did not help that he had difficulty in paying them for their support. He was in trouble with Parliament in England, and there were many in his southern realm who regarded the Scots as their truest allies and who, consequently, would not draw a sword against them.

Royal pride—and the evidence of it was never hard to find in Charles—had to be swallowed. The king who had come to intimidate and to conquer was forced by circumstances to negotiate terms of peace. Under the Pacification of Berwick—for so the resultant treaty was called—Charles agreed to call a free Assembly and free Parliament to settle the affairs of Scotland. But the concession was made under pressure of circumstances over which he had lost all control. It was secured—as a wit of the times put it—"not under bishops' law, nor under canon law, but under *Dunse Law!*"

When the promised free Assembly and free Parliament met in Edinburgh in August 1639 the decisions reached were altogether favourable to the Covenanters. Episcopacy was again put down and Presbyterianism established as the polity of the Scottish Church. But the king had not changed his mind. Just as he had refused to accept the decisions of the Glasgow Assembly of the previous year, so now he spurned the findings of the free Assembly and the free Parliament which had been called with his own agreement.

But if Charles was determined, so too were the Covenanters. Using the advantage that still lay with them they invaded England so as to prevent the king from invading Scotland. Winning an easy victory over the Royalists they marched into Newcastle and took up quarters there. Eventually, in 1641, a treaty was made at Westminster under which the demands of the Covenanters were met.

But—

> He that complies against his will
> Is of the same opinion still.

For even while he was in negotiation with the upholders of Scottish Presbyterianism, Charles wrote to Archbishop Spottiswoode, the leader of Scottish Episcopacy, to say, "You may rest secure that, though perhaps we may give way for the present to that which be prejudicial to the Church and our Government, yet we shall not leave thinking in time how to remedy both."[2]

Events south of the Border continued to influence the course of the struggle for freedom which was proceeding in Scotland. Charles fully shared his father's belief that "as to dispute what

22

God may do is blasphemy, so is to dispute what a king may do in the height of his power." It was this belief that brought him into collision with the Church in Scotland and with Parliament in England, and in their straits the oppressed parties in the two countries proposed that "a strict union and league" be entered into between them in defence of religion and liberty. This league—*The Solemn League and Covenant* as it was called—was drafted by Alexander Henderson and signed in St. Margaret's Church, Westminster, on 25th September 1643. On the 13th day of the following month it was signed in Edinburgh amidst scenes of great joy and thanksgiving.

The attractions that such a bond had for the Scottish Presbyterians are obvious. The unity and stability of the two kingdoms could best be assured by an agreement relating to faith and order. Alexander Henderson, in his manual on *The Government and Order of the Church of Scotland,* published in 1641, had described Presbyterianism as a recognition of "superiority without tyranny, parity without confusion and disorder, and subjection without slavery," and there was much in Presbyterianism that attracted the Reforming party in the Church of England. Charles too was fully awake to the advantage of ecclesiastical uniformity as a unifying and stabilising influence in days of political intrigue and party strife, and having failed to establish it on a High Anglican basis he gave the impression that he might be willing, if only for an experimental period, to give way to the Presbyterian alternative. But expediency and opportunism entered far too deeply into the planning. True it is that

> *"misery acquaints a man with strange bed-fellows."*

And when the misery which brings into being this association of dissimilars is ended, or even alleviated, the tendency is for the parties who were brought together under its pressure to resume their separate ways.

So it happened in the case of the *Solemn League and Covenant.* The aims of the Scottish planners were good, and the terms of the Covenant which they submitted as the basis of the proposed League were in no way derogatory to royal authority properly exercised. They aimed at bringing the national established churches "to the nearest conjunction and uniformity in Religion, Confession of Faith, Form of Church government, Directory for Worship and Catechizing;" and "mutually to preserve the rights and privileges of the Parliaments, and the liberties of the kingdoms; and to preserve and defend the King's Majesty's person and authority, in the preservation and defence of the true religion and liberties of the kingdoms; that the world may bear witness with our consciences of our loyalty, and that we have no thoughts or intentions to diminish his Majesty's just power and greatness."[3]

This was no rebel bond, but a careful reassertion of Melville's doctrine of the "two kings and two kingdoms"; with a salutary reminder that the true Divine Right of Kings must always be seen to accord with the Word of Him by Whom "kings reign, and princes decree justice."

The achievement of religious uniformity, however, requires that the bond subscribed to that end, as well as expressing the deep convictions of those who enter into it, must also be voluntarily taken. The difference between the English Parliamentarians and the Scottish Covenanters in this regard was neatly hit off by Robert Baillie. "The English," he wrote, "were for a civil League; we for a religious Covenant." The result was predictable. When the battle of Naseby in 1645 gave them their decisive victory over the Royalist forces the zeal of the English Parliamentarians for the *Solemn League and Covenant* immediately abated, and the pressure which had been exerted upon them by the Scots in that connection was made a ground of accusation against them. They were imitating the king, it was said, against whose oppressive methods they had gone into revolt in their own country. "New presbyter," taunted Milton, "is old priest writ large."[4]

But the attempt to find an acceptable confessional basis for the Churches concerned in the League had one outstandingly notable result. The historic Westminster Assembly of Divines began its sittings in 1643 and continued to meet for six years. And notwithstanding its failure to accomplish all that was envisaged in the *Solemn League and Covenant,* it justified its long and laborious existence by the documents which it produced, pre-eminent among them the *Westminster Confession of Faith* which is second to none among Reformed Confessions, and which became the principal subordinate standard of Presbyterianism throughout the world. It represents a sincere effort to reform the church by the regulative principle of Holy Scripture. Every member of the Assembly was required to take the following vow; "I do seriously promise and vow, in the presence of Almighty God, that in this Assembly whereof I am a member, I will maintain nothing in point of doctrine but what I believe to be most agreeable to the Word of God; nor in point of discipline, but what may make most for God's glory, and the peace and good of His Church." And while the spiritual independence of the Church is fully claimed and safeguarded, so too is the office of the civil magistrate within his own province. Church and State, as the twin provinces of Christ's Kingdom, must seek each other's benefit, helping one another in the discharge of the duties assigned them by the King to Whom they are alike answerable; and respecting each other's rights and privileges according to the teaching of the Statute Book of His realm, the Word of God.

The axe that executed Charles I by that same stroke cut asunder the Scottish Covenanters and the English Parliamentarians. Formerly associates in a struggle for freedom they were now divided into hostile camps. Scotland indeed had little cause to mourn the fate of Charles, but old loyalties die hard. He was one of themselves; furthermore, for the most part, they were monarchists at heart, and anything savouring of republicanism was foreign to their liking. There were qualities in Charles that appealed to them, and they kept hoping to the end that he might be persuaded to exercise his royal authority in ways that would give due recognition to the rights of the people. At the king's invitation, Alexander Henderson had gone to Newcastle to confer with him. But there is no reasoning with an obstinate man whose mind is under thrall to a fixed idea. From the political philosophy which he had learned from his father no argument could budge him. "I would say without hyperbole," he insisted, "that there was not a wiser man since Solomon, than he who said 'No Bishop, No King.'" And that was that! In the upholding of that dominating principle the end justified the means! "Charles," says Dr. King Hewison, "was an incorrigible liar, and to his mendacity may be traced all his own personal afflictions as well as the woes which his perfidy brought on his unhappy kingdom." "Nothing in life became him, like the leaving it" was Andrew Lang's doubtful panegyric on him. Yet when the tidings of his execution reached Scotland his subjects there were horrified. Twice their former allies in England had broken faith with them; first, over the *Solemn League and Covenant,* and now over the life of the king; for he had been handed over to the Parliamentary Commissioners on the understanding that no harm was to be done to his person.

Within a week of the king's execution the Scots proclaimed his son, Charles II, at the Mercat Cross of Edinburgh. Cromwell invaded Scotland and routed the Covenanting army at Dunbar. But the leaders of the Covenanters refused to acknowledge defeat, and Charles was crowned at Scone on the 1st of January, 1651. On the 3rd of September in the same year, and exactly a year after his victory at Dunbar, Cromwell won his decisive victory over the Scottish army at Worcester, and Charles, now destitute of military support, had again to seek refuge on the Continent.

During the years of Cromwell's supremacy Scotland was treated very much as a conquered province, yet the Church enjoyed a considerable measure of freedom. True, the General Assembly was suppressed, but in other respects the Church was given liberty of faith and practice. Kirk-sessions, presbyteries and synods were permitted to meet as usual. It was a period when the Spirit of God was manifestly outpoured upon the Church. The Word was preached without let or hindrance, and James Kirkton the historian gives us the following account of the changed Scotland which emerged under the Protectorate.

"At the King's return every paroche had a minister, every village had a school, every family almost had a Bible, yea, in most of the countrey, all the children of age could read the Scriptures. Every minister was oblieged to preach thrice a week, to lecture and catechise once, besides other private duties wherein they abounded, according to their proportion of faithfulness and abilities. . . . In many places the Spirit seemed to be powerd out with the Word both by the multitude of sincere converts, and also by the common work of reformation upon many who never came the length of a Communion; there were no fewer than sixty aged people, men and women, who went to school, that even then they might be able to read the Scriptures with their own eyes. I have lived many years in a paroche where I have never heard ane oath, and you have ridde many miles before you heard any. Also you could not, for a great part of the countrey, have lodged in a family where the Lord was not worshipped by reading, singing, and publick prayer. Nobody complained more of our Church government than our taverners, whose ordinarie lamentation was, their trade was broke, people were become so sober."

The rich crop of converts to which Kirkton refers was to provide holy fuel for martyr fires in the Killing Times that followed the Restoration.

1. J. King Hewison, *The Covenanters*, vol. 1; p. 287.
2. ibid. pp. 331, 332.
3. J. Douglas, *Light in the North;* pp. 206, 207.
4. T. Ratcliffe Barnett, *The Story of the Covenant;* p. 61.
5. J. King Hewison, *The Covenanters*, vol. 1; p. 369.
6. J. Kirkton, *History of the Church of Scotland;* pp. 64, 65.

CHAPTER FIVE

THE END OF A DYNASTY

His guide was not duty; it was not even ambition; but his guide was self; it was ease, and amusement, and lust.—Osmund Airy, on Charles II.

In the recall of Charles II from exile in 1660 after the collapse of Cromwell's Protectorate the Scottish people had taken their full share, but their loyalty was ill-requited. The unreliability of his father and grandfather was reproduced in Charles and while he undoubtedly had some shining gifts of kingcraft he was utterly unscrupulous. His promise, given at his coronation at Scone in 1651, that he would support Presbyterianism and "have no enemies but the enemies of the Covenant, and no friends but the friends of the Covenant," had long since been forgotten. A thorough profligate who impoverished his country in order to provide for his many mistresses and illegitimate children, the cause of true religion could expect no support from him. His interest in Episcopacy was a necessity of government. The Church was a force that had to be reckoned with, and the best way of securing control of it was to have the final word in its affairs. Episcopacy had proved itself more pliable and manageable than Presbyterianism, therefore the rule of the bishops must be restored. "Presbyterianism," he said, "was no religion for a gentleman." Its moral code repelled him; for its discipline he had nothing but ridicule and contempt. "He minded nothing but his pleasures," laments Samuel Pepys who himself had some addiction to the same kind of "pleasures" notwithstanding the religiosity with which he was wont to express himself.

Believing that a monarch had a Divine right to rule as he pleased, Charles ruthlessly put down everything that he regarded as a challenge to his power. His "Drunken Parliament," as it was rightly called, passed an Act of Supremacy making the king supreme in all affairs of Church and State. It became high treason to deny his absolute authority. An Act Recissory was passed repealing "all the Acts and deeds passed and done" in the Parliaments that had sat between 1640 and 1648. The *National Covenant* and the *Solemn League and Covenant* were declared to be unlawful oaths and no longer binding, and the government of the Church was claimed as a prerogative of the Crown. It was enacted that Episcopacy should be the form of church government in Scotland.

27

This change necessitated the appointment of new bishops. James Sharp of Crail, was one of those sent up to London to represent the cause of the Scottish Church, but Sharp used the occasion to further his own interests, and he returned to Scotland eventually to become the Archbishop of St. Andrews. With tigerish ferocity he now turned against his former brethren and was directly responsible for much of the brutal persecution that they had to endure. Singling out James Guthrie of Stirling, George Gillespie of Kirkcaldy, and Samuel Rutherford of St. Andrews as the "leading impostors", he urged the Earl of Lauderdale, who was the King's Secretary in Scotland, to exercise "great severity" upon them, and thereby "daunt the rest of the hot-heads."

Guthrie alone of the three mentioned by Sharp came to a martyr's death. Frail George Gillespie, who had given such excellent service at the Westminster Assembly of Divines, died a natural death. Rutherford, whose treatise on the duties of Prince and People—*Lex Rex*—was so uncompromisingly opposed to Stewart absolutism, would certainly have sealed his testimony with his blood but for the fact that he was already a dying man when the summons to trial before Parliament reached him. But the ministry of the Church generally did not consist of such timid time-servers as Sharp had imagined, for when the Privy Council at Sharp's instigation enacted in 1662 the banishment from their parishes of all the ministers who had been admitted since 1649 unless they obtained a presentation to their parishes from the patron, and collation from the bishop of the diocese, almost four-hundred of these ministers sacrificed their worldly interests rather than their spiritual freedom.

The charges thus rendered vacant were filled by the appointment to them, for the most part, of men spiritually as well as educationally unfit to serve in the Christian ministry. Bishop Gilbert Burnet, although he always described himself as "completely episcopal," speaks of them as "a disgrace to their orders," and "the dregs and refuse of the northern parts."[1] It was not surprising that multitudes of the people refused to hear the "bishops' curates" as they were derisively called, and preferred to share the risks and discomforts of their "outed" pastors. Crippling fines and penalties were laid upon them by an Act of Parliament—mockingly called the Bishops' Dragnet—but Sharp and his fellow-persecutors who thought that the people could be intimidated and subdued by such measures completely miscalculated their temper. It has been judged that by his ruthless intolerance James Sharp advanced the cause of the Presbyterianism from which he had defected more than that of the Episcopacy to which he had gone over.

In 1669 a royal Indulgence was issued permitting the "outed" ministers who had given no trouble, to return to their parishes, or, if these were not vacant, to accept appointment to other parishes on terms that they might find easy to comply with. Some forty ministers availed themselves of this leniency, and thereby gave rise to a new difficulty. The Indulgence was an act of sheer absolutism, over-riding all civil and ecclesiastical law, and the ministers who accepted it thereby put themselves into the position that they held their parishes, not by any ecclesiastical process, either Presbyterian or Episcopalian, but simply by an arbitrary act of government. The result was that the indulged ministers became a separate class within the Church under the absolute jurisdiction of the State.

The struggle of the people to safeguard the spiritual independence of the Church continued. It is needless to recapitulate here, even in the briefest outline, the atrocities of those years, perpetrated in the name of good government. The monuments studded over the Covenanting martyrland, from the massive memorial stone in Greyfriars Churchyard in Edinburgh, where many of them were buried after their execution in the Grassmarket nearby, to the solitary grave at Priesthill near the spot where John Brown was shot before his wife's eyes, and the stone-shaft in the waters of the Solway where young Margaret Wilson was drowned with a Psalm on her lips after having witnessed the death of her elderly companion Margaret Lachlison in the swirling tide which was so soon to set her free to be "with Christ, which is far better"—all these are silent but impressive memorials to heroic souls of all ranks and ages who "overcame by the blood of the Lamb, and by the word of their testimony; and loved not their lives unto the death."

For twenty-eight years the brutal persecution continued until, according to a widely accepted—but perhaps exaggerated —reckoning, over 18,000 people fell victims to the blood-lust of an evil confederacy of statesmen and churchmen who were set on binding the Church of Jesus Christ to the vassalage of royal tyrants who claimed to be exercising a Divine Right even when they were imbruing their hands in the blood of God's children. James Stewart, Duke of York, as King's Commissioner, declared that order could never be restored until "all the south side of the Forth were made a hunting-ground." And a veritable hunting-ground it became.

James VII succeeded to the throne on the death of his brother, Charles II, in 1685. For Charles no more honest epitaph could have been composed than is provided in the pronouncement of his fellow-Episcopalian, Bishop Gilbert Burnet. "A secularist," writes Burnet, "he shook off Presbyterianism as a viper, utilised Episcopacy as the readiest political tool, and finally put on Popery as a comfortable shroud to die in."[2] James was at least more consistent in his religious attachment. A Roman Catholic he was, and a Roman Catholic he was determined to remain. Not only so, he was fully resolved to rehabilitate Roman Catholicism throughout his realm. Louis XIV of France had revoked the Edict of Nantes in 1685 as a final measure in the repression of the Huguenots. What had succeeded in France might well prove successful in Scotland. But with a dash of Stewart diplomacy he represented himself as an advocate of religious toleration. The change in role was too sudden not to be suspect, and it soon became only too obvious that the "toleration" he had in mind was meant to help chiefly the hard-pressed cause of the papacy in his realm. When, therefore, in 1686 he asked the Scottish Parliament to repeal the laws which bore against Roman Catholics he met with resistance.

The king now turned to intensive propaganda. The Chapel at Holyrood was laid out for worship in the Roman form. A printing press was installed, and Jesuits were employed to disseminate Roman Catholic doctrine from Holyrood. Protestants were removed from various prominent offices and replaced by Roman Catholics, and a policy of infiltration gathered strength. In 1687 James issued—entirely on his own authority—two proclamations of Indulgence, the first of which permitted Presbyterians to worship in their own way, but in private houses only; while at the same time the laws against Roman Catholics were suspended. The second Indulgence suspended the penal laws against non-conformity to the religion established by law, and permission was given to all to worship in their chosen way, provided that notification of the preachers and the places of meeting were made known to the local authorities, and that no disloyal sentiments be uttered. The laws against conventicles remained unchanged, and the king's general behaviour showed clearly that no legal rights formerly recognised were now immune from invasion. But he committed a fatal blunder when he committed Archbishop Sancroft and six other bishops for trial because they had declined to support his autocratic demand that the declaration of Indulgence, issued in 1688, should be read in all the churches. The imprisoned bishops immediately became national heroes, and their acquittal was greeted with widespread demonstrations of support for the position which they had taken. The king's despotic action had the effect of opening the eyes of the people to the true character of his policy, and he was widely held to have forfeited his right to the throne.

The tyranny of James had far-reaching results for the religious life of the whole country. Protestants of all shades drew closer together in their resistance to Romanist intrigue and royalist autocracy and the position of dissenters generally was considerably eased. James Stewart's grand plan for the restoration of Roman Catholicism in his realm had the effect, that a wiser man would have foreseen, of uniting his subjects against himself and accomplishing the downfall of the dynasty which had brought the land of its origin near to destruction. Even the long-favoured supporters of Episcopacy decided that the concentration of all power in the hands of one man, king though he might be, was more than could be allowed by the nation, especially when Protestantism was put in peril of its very existence. Even James could now read the signs of the times, and he saw that they boded no good for him and his house.

On 5th November 1688, William of Orange landed at Torbay with an army to claim the throne, and James Stewart, who had made fugitives of so many of the best people in his realm, became a fugitive himself. On 10th December 1688, in heavy disguise, and with no better transport than a miserable fishing boat, he crossed the Channel by night to find sanctuary in Roman Catholic France where he still hoped to rally assistance for the recapturing of his throne for the house of Stewart, and his dominions for the Church of Rome.

1. Gilbert Burnet, *History of our own Time,* vol. 1; p. 221.
2. ibid. vol. 2; p. 464.

CHAPTER SIX

THE REVOLUTION

The name "Moderate" has every recommendation but
that of being descriptive. —*Lord Lorne.*

The action of the Covenanters in resisting the king by armed
force has given their detractors their opportunity to stigmatise
them as rebels, and has led many who sympathised with their
aims to deplore their defiance of constituted authority. But it is
only too easy to misjudge these champions of spiritual freedom. If
they revolted it was because Charles I had compelled them.
Nowhere in his dominions did he have more loyal subjects than in
Scotland; indeed, the attachment of the Scottish people to the ill-
starred house of the Stewarts was almost foolish in its intensity.
Willingly, they rendered to Caesar the things that were Caesar's,
but when they were commanded to render unto Caesar that which
was Christ's their supreme loyalty asserted itself, and they banded
together in defence of their spiritual heritage, and for the honour
of Christ the King and Head of the Church. "Fanatics and
rebels" was Andrew Lang's judgment of them, confronting the
government with demands that it could not in reason grant. All
that the government desired, especially in the latter stages of the
conflict, was (according to Lang) "to keep the Presbyterians in as
good order as Cromwell had done." But a dispassionate
comparison of the ecclesiastical policy of Cromwell with that of
the Stewart monarchs will readily show the difference between
Lang's judgment and the verdict of history. Whatever the defects
of Cromwell's administration, apart from his suppression of the
General Assembly he made no attempt to deprive the Church of
its spiritual independence, and Scotland experienced rich spiritual
blessing during the period of his Protectorate.

Under the Stewarts the situation was very different. Indeed,
Charles II all but succeeded in transforming Scotland into a
totalitarian despotism. Only the Church, or rather a resolute
minority within the Church, stood between him and the
realisation of his purpose. As the true successors of Knox and his
fellow Reformers they took the view that the power of the ruler
was derived from the people. For royal absolutism they could find
no authority in Holy Scripture, nor did it agree with the canons of
good government. Knox had been characteristically outspoken in
this regard. "Think you," Queen Mary demanded in one of their

stormy interviews, "that subjects, having the power, may resist their princes?"

"If princes exceed their power, Madam," replied Knox, "no doubt they may be resisted, even by power. For no greater honour is to be given to kings than God has commanded to be given to father and mother. But the father may be struck with a frenzy, in which he would slay his children. Now, Madam, if the children arise, join together, apprehend the father, take the sword from him, bind his hands, and keep him in prison till the frenzy is over, think you, Madam, that the children do any wrong? Even so, Madam, it is with princes that would murder the children of God that are subject to them."[1]

The Church, as Melville had so plainly told James VI, was not a department of the State, and its spiritual jurisdiction must never be usurped by the State. Yet the *King's Confession,* the *National Covenant,* and the *Solemn League and Covenant* all bound the signatories to a loyal support of the King and a faithful recognition of his authority and defence of his person. But consistently they opposed encroachment upon the prerogatives of Christ as Head of the Church, from whatever quarter the threat might come. Just as they opposed the encroachments of the Stewarts, so they did the encroachments of Cromwell. For when Colonel Cotterall, as the Protector's representative, intruded upon the General Assembly held in Edinburgh in July 1653, and demanded to know by whose authority they had gathered, the Moderator, David Dickson, replied, "We sit, not as having authority from any power on earth, but as having power and authority from Jesus Christ; and by Him, and for Him, and for the good of His Church." And when in the following year Cromwell tempted the Protesting party in the Church with the control of ecclesiastical affairs in Scotland, the offer was rejected on the ground that it constituted an encroachment by the State on the jurisdiction of the Church courts.

These men prized their freedom. They had won it dearly, and they were prepared to maintain it even at the cost of sufferings and death.

The stricter Covenanters, the Cameronians—so named after their intrepid leader, Richard Cameron—had all along held to the lawfulness of "defensive war", and they justified their resort to arms on that ground. In June 1680 they posted their *Declaration* at Sanquhar, rejecting the authority of Charles II, and, judging the Stewart monarchy to be beyond reform, they decided on revolution. The *Queensferry Paper,* which has been described as the most intransigent of Covenanting manifestoes, indicates the lines on which their minds were working. Not only did they declare for the withdrawing of allegiance from the Stewarts but they pronounced against hereditary monarchy altogether. Further, they regarded "government by a single person being most liable to inconveniences, and aptest to degenerate into tyranny, as long and sad experience hath taught us."[2] They envisaged a new commonwealth, rather on republican lines, and moulded on ancient Israel. The document ends on a monitory note, declaring that if the present persecution should continue they would regard the situation as one of war, and would prosecute the conflict resolutely in defence of their rights. It was inevitable that in more settled times they should be regarded as extremists, but we do them less than justice if we fail to recognise that it is to these "outlaws for freedom,"[3] as Dr Hector Macpherson describes them, that we owe the concept of freedom in Church and State that is basic to our democracy.

The last preacher-martyr of Covenanting times went to the stake on 17th February 1688 with the dew of his youth still fresh upon him; for James Renwick was only twenty-six years of age when his final testimony was required of him. Less than seven years previously he had witnessed the martyrdom of Donald Cargill, and, far from being unnerved by the sight, he resolved that the cause for which Cargill had given his life must be the one to which he should give whole-hearted service, cost what it might. It was a brief but gallant ministry, and it ended in a glow of splendour. He went to the scaffold rejoicing that he was judged worthy to suffer such a fate—"an honour not shared by the angels." Even from the scaffold he rallied his friends and followers, and expressed his confidence for the future. "Keep your ground," he cried, "and the Lord will provide you teachers and ministers. And when He comes He will make these despised truths glorious in the earth."[4]

The time of the expected deliverance was nearer than appeared on that cold day in February.

William and Mary were King and Queen of England for a year before similar recognition was accorded them in Scotland. From the outset, it was made clear to William that his occupancy of the throne would at all times be conditional upon his compliance in government with the laws of the land, and that no changes could be made in those laws without the consent of Parliament. The regal absolutism claimed by the later Stewarts must be regarded as ended for ever.

William's early advisers were Anglicans, and, although he himself was a Presbyterian, he was plainly warned that he must avoid giving offence to the Episcopalians, upon whose support his tenure of the English throne so largely depended. At the same time, he must be careful not to prejudice his position with the Presbyterians of Scotland who had shown so decisively that no form of Church government would satisfy them but one that did justice to the spiritual independence of the Church within her own domain, implying the right of congregations to choose their own pastors. William knew that the Presbyterians were his truest support in Scotland, and that the Scottish bishops remained Jacobite in their loyalty. Altogether, the situation required more diplomacy and statecraft than William could as yet bring to bear upon it.

The fact that a settlement so widely agreeable to the Scottish people was achieved by 1690 was largely due to the political sagacity and experienced churchmanship of William Carstares. Carstares, a Scotsman and a son of the manse, had shared in the sufferings of Scotland's persecuted Church. He had been imprisoned and tortured, and, when eventually he was banished to the Continent, in a very literal sense he bore in his body the marks of the Lord Jesus, for his hands were permanently disfigured and mutilated by the thumb-screws which his torturers had used in their endeavours to extract information from him. In his banishment he became the trusted friend of William of Orange, and when the Dutch Prince landed in Torbay with his army in 1688, Carstares accompanied him as his chaplain and secretary. Many mistrusted him. To them he was an arch-type of the "wily ecclesiastic." The Jacobites dubbed him "Cardinal" Carstares. But King William thought differently of his counsellor. "I have known William Carstares long," he said, "I have known him well, and I know him as an honest man." The bond between the two Williams served Scotland well. The Protestantism of William of Orange was above suspicion, but his convictions in matters of ecclesiastical government were weak and indeterminate. An Erastian at heart, he would fain have claimed a fuller control of Church affairs. But danger signals confronted him, and if at any time he did not fully understand them, Carstares was always at hand to make their meaning plain. When, on one occasion, in Carstares' absence, and on the ill-advice of Lord Stair and Lord Tarbat, the king sent an inflammatory despatch to Scotland that would have caused a revolt against him, Carstares had the temerity to intercept the courier and relieve him of his dangerous missive, thereafter seeking an immediate audience of the king to confess to his deed and surrender his life if the king insisted on having his way. The measure of the king's confidence in Carstares is indicated in the fact that he condoned his action and destroyed the despatch—a directive which stipulated the conditions on which ministers would be admitted to membership of the Church's Courts, and which gave both King and Parliament the right to interpose in affairs that were purely ecclesiastical. Such Erastian intervention would have been regarded as a glaring encroachment on the Church's cherished spiritual independence, and would have weakened William's rule in Scotland. The king was firmly reminded that the spiritual independence of the Church was a matter on which his Presbyterian subjects in Scotland were not prepared to compromise.

"Wily Willie" they may have called Carstares, but we have the highest authority for believing that the wisdom of the serpent and the harmlessness of the dove is not an incongruous association!

The Revolution Settlement which was effected in 1690 was an honest endeavour to establish ecclesiastical peace in circumstances of extreme difficulty. Episcopacy was abolished; the survivors of the 400 ministers expelled from their livings in 1662 were reinstated; the Act of 1592 — the "Magna Carta of Presbyterianism"—was restored; the *Westminster Confession* was ratified as the standard of the Church's belief; patronage was abolished, the right of choosing a minister being given to the elders and heritors, or land-owners, but with the congregation having the right to appeal to the Presbytery of the bounds against the settlement of a minister to whom they objected. The Episcopalian ministers were allowed to stay in their charges, provided they took an oath of allegiance and accepted Presbyterian government. The General Assembly resumed its former position of authority, although the right of calling it was still left with the king.

When the General Assembly met in 1690 it was the first such gathering for thirty-seven years. In his message to the Assembly the king urged upon the members "a calm and peaceable procedure" as being "no less pleasing to us than it becometh you. . . . Moderation is what religion enjoins, neighbouring Churches expect of you, and we recommend to you."[5] On the whole, the Assembly inclined to the irenical approach which William desiderated, but the Cameronians would have preferred stronger measures in the preservation and advancement of Presbyterianism, and were particularly displeased by the omission of the Covenants from the Revolution Settlement. Accordingly, they took no further part in the settlement of the affairs of the Scottish Church. Their Societies continued their separate existence until, having been joined by two presbyterially ordained ministers, they constituted the Reformed Presbyterian Church in 1743.

That there were indeed elements of weakness in the Revolution Settlement soon became widely evident. There were several ministers in the Church who had accepted the royal Indulgence under James VII and they certainly were not regarded as heroes by their more resolute brethren. Furthermore, many of the

Episcopalian clergy, availing themselves of the conditions offered by the Church to those who desired to continue in the parishes which they had served prior to the Revolution, changed to Presbyterianism. Some indeed continued in their pastoral charges without fulfilling the stipulated conditions, and no action was taken against them. Strength of loyalty and conviction could hardly be looked for in such a heterogeneous ministry. The "Moderates" among them were numerous, and the party-name was of their own choosing. Their teaching has been described as "a Gospel without grace, setting forth salvation by works."[6] But if they preached "good works" there was more than a grain of truth in the remark of the cynic who said that "they left it to others to perform them."

Lord Cockburn thus describes the typical Moderate; "His clay was perfectly impervious to the deep and fervid spirit which is the soul of modern religion."

The defenders and successors of the Moderates in more modern times—for their race is not extinct, although their early designation has fallen into disuse—speak of them as modest men, not presuming to expound the more profound doctrines of the faith as their "highflyer" opposites in the Evangelical party did; men of balance and restraint, of good breeding and wide culture who could meet on equal terms with the intelligentsia of the day and be thoroughly at home among them. And much of this must be allowed. Moderatism indeed had its distinctive culture, but it was not the authentic culture of Calvary. Thomas Chalmers had once belonged to their number, and was thereby well qualified to assess them, and this is his comment on their preaching: "A Moderate sermon is like a winter's day, short and clear, and cold. The brevity is good; the clarity is better; the coldness is fatal. Moonlight preaching ripens no harvests."[6]

That the king should favour this party in the Church was to be expected. Their very pliancy was, from his viewpoint, an advantage, if only a temporary one. For William, a thorough Erastian always, desired to have more of a say in Church affairs than the true Presbyterians were prepared to allow. But these were a minority in the post-Revolution Church, and it suited the king's policy to have, as the dominant party in the General Assembly, men who would cede to him the measure of control that he desired. In his eagerness to realise this purpose he went beyond the bounds of prudence and urged an easier admission to the ministry of the Church of the former supporters of Episcopacy. The Presbyterians, however, felt that they had exceeded the limits of prudence and charity in the measure of moderation which, in response to the king's request, they had already shown. The men for whom the king was pleading had

37

recently been their persecutors, and the readiness of so many of them to change to a modified Presbyterian order was brought about by considerations of political advantage rather than by any genuine change of convictions. Moreover, signs were not lacking that what they were really after was not equality in the Church but a definite ascendancy, yet without committing themselves to an oath of loyalty to William, or to a promise of obedience to Presbyterian government. William's tenure of the throne still seemed insecure. Subversive action by an influential Jacobite faction was a constant menace. Uncommitted to William by any oath of loyalty, the Prelatist party in the Church would find it easy to resume their Jacobite attachment. And uncommitted to Presbyterianism by any definite pledge, their reversion to the rule of the bishops would present no obstacle. That their policy was one of pure opportunism was not unknown to the king; but to hold his position with the Episcopalians of both England and Scotland he must be careful that he should not appear to show undue favour to the Scottish Presbyterians, especially since he was a Presbyterian himself.

For the emergence of Moderatism in the Church the royal policy was primarily to blame, but the Church herself cannot be exculpated, and her failure to ensure that her inherent principles were adequately safeguarded was to involve her in much controversy and strife in days to come. At the same time, the answer must be given to those who tend to represent the Revolution Settlement as wholly Erastian and the Church herself as abandoning fundamental principle, that in 1698 the General Assembly, in answer to the Cameronians, issued a document, known as *A Seasonable Admonition*, in which they declared; "We do believe and own that Jesus Christ is the only Head and King of His Church; and that He hath instituted in His Church, officers and ordinances, order and government, and not left it to the will of man, magistrate, or Church, to alter at their pleasure. And we believe that this government is neither prelatical nor congregational, but Presbyterian, which now, through the mercy of God, is established among us; and we believe we have a better foundation for this our church government than the inclination of the people or the laws of men."

The old aim emerges clearly, the determination to preserve inviolate the democratic government of the Church under the sole Headship of Jesus Christ.

1. T. McCrie, *Sketches of Church History,* vol. 1; pp. 82, 83.
2. J. C. Johnston, *Treasury of the Covenant;* p. 138.
3. H. Macpherson, *Outlaws for Freedom;* p. 119 et seq.
4. J. Howie, *The Scots Worthies* (Bonar edn.); p. 575.
5. H. Watt, *Thomas Chalmers and the Disruption;* p. 6.

CHAPTER SEVEN

THE RESTORATION OF PATRONAGE

Shall we suppose that God granted to any set of men —
patrons, heritors, elders, or whatever they may be — a
power to impose servants on His family without their
consent, being the freest society in the world? —
Ebenezer Erskine.

King William died in 1702, seven years after the death of his wife. There being no children, the crown passed to Princess Anne, Mary's sister, who, at her accession, gave the stipulated assurance of protection for Presbyterian Church government in Scotland. In 1707, at the Union of the Parliaments of England and Scotland, the legislation covering the event was so fashioned as to safeguard the Scottish Church's position. The continuity of her Presbyterian government was guaranteed by the Act of Union, and the coronation engagements of each successive sovereign included an oath that he, or she, would protect the government, worship, discipline, rights and privileges of the national Church of Scotland.

But political promises are notoriously brittle, as the Church had already proved at bitter cost. Jacobite intrigue was still rife, and Queen Anne herself was not opposed to it. She had always hated her brother-in-law, King William, and had frequent spasms of remorse for having acquiesced in the dethronement of her father. The prospect of a German succession to the throne added to her grief and made the restoration of the Stewarts all the more an event to be favoured. The Jacobite party were still committed to their restoration policy, and it suited their purpose to bring the Scottish Church into collision with the Government. Consequently, they coalesced with the High Church party and the Tories to bring about the passing, in 1712, of an Act which, in flagrant violation of the Act of Union, re-imposed Patronage on the Scottish Church. "The toleration of Episcopalians, and the restoration of Patronage," declares Principal R. H. Story in his *Life of William Carstares,* "were advocated for the sole purpose of regaining their lost ascendancy to the Episcopalians and Jacobites of Scotland."[1]

The Queen favoured the measure, for it was in line with her policy "to make Churchmen more dependent on the aristocracy."

To begin with, however, the Patronage Act had little effect on the general life of the Church. The call of the people and the concurrence of the Presbytery of the bounds were still necessary to the effecting of a pastoral settlement. If therefore the patron's nominee was unacceptable to the people he could be set aside. But unscrupulous patrons could turn this arrangement to their own advantage. By presenting unacceptable men they could prolong the vacancy in the pastorate and use for their own purposes the money that ought to go to the payment of the minister's stipend. This infamous Bill, rushed through at such speed that the Scottish Church had little opportunity to organise effective opposition to it, was, on the estimate of Lord Moncrieff, "directly in violation of that solemn engagement, on the faith of which alone the union of the kingdoms was passed." Many of the patrons were Episcopalian, and the fear that they might use their rights of presentation to the advancement of party interests was not groundless, as after events proved. "Whether the hand of the misguided Sovereign shook when affixing the sign manual," writes Professor W. H. Hetherington, "has not been recorded; but certainly at that moment she put her hand to a deed by which her right to reign was virtually rescinded, the Revolution Settlement overturned, and the Treaty of Union repealed; unless, indeed, the Bill itself were to be regarded as an absolute nullity — an idle arrangement of mere words, 'full of sound and fury, signifying nothing'."[2]

The General Assembly following the passing of the Patronage Act communicated to the Queen their disapproval of the recent legislation, which they described as "grievous and prejudicial to this Church." They instructed their Commission to use all proper means to have the Act repealed, and renewed the instruction annually for many years thereafter. But patronage remained, and the patrons rapidly grew in influence. Soon it was claimed that a call to a minister, signed only by the heritors and elders, was sufficient, as against the view that it should have the support of the heads of families in the membership of the congregation concerned. It was not long until even that limited measure of popular acquiescence came to be virtually discounted, and the nomination by the patron alone was held to suffice. It was on this ground that a licentiate, presented to Burntisland by the Queen in 1715, but opposed by the people, took his stand and claimed his right to be ordained and inducted to the charge. But the Assembly's reaction was swift and decisive; the protester was deprived of his licence.

Ten years later the magistrates and town council of Aberdeen who, as heritors, had the right along with the elders to propose a minister to a vacant charge in the city, decided to go further, and make an absolute ministerial appointment without regard to the wishes of the people. The Synod disapproved of their action, and the magistrates appealed to the General Assembly. The decision of the Assembly was that a new call should be drawn up, and that the inclinations of the heads of families in the congregation be ascertained. When this was done, 139 heads of families voted for the presentee, and 307 voted against him. The call, nevertheless, was sustained by the Commission to whom the matter had been remitted, several members expressing their dissent.

Evangelical ministers found little favour with the patrons, for they were recognised as men of influence with the people. Thomas Boston, for example, one of Scotland's ablest and saintliest ministers, had great difficulty in obtaining a pastoral charge, not because the congregations to whom he preached were not attracted to him, but because — as he puts it — "some that had the greatest power were against me, as it ordinarily fared with me in the places where I used to preach."

In some cases where the Presbyteries refused to induct the patron's presentee because the congregation had indicated their opposition to the proposed settlement, the General Assembly, now under the domination of a Moderate majority, took the matter out of their hands and appointed a committee of their own to induct the unwanted presentee, at the same time permitting any member of Presbytery who might so desire to take part in the proceedings. Such "Riding Committees" as they were called, were an obvious violation of Presbyterian order, and their activities had the effect of strengthening the opposition of the people to the party in the Assembly by whose connivance they were being deprived of their rights and privileges in the Church of Christ. But when the Evangelical party gave expression to their grievances their remonstrances were treated by the Assembly as censurable.

Obviously, the Church was heading for a crisis, and when it came it was associated with the honoured name of Ebenezer Erskine. Erskine, the son of Henry Erskine, of Chirnside — a Covenanter minister who had endured much persecution for the Gospel — had acquired wide popularity as a preacher during his ministry at Portmoak. During that period, and before his removal to Stirling in 1731, a vacancy occurred in Kinross, and the people desired to call Erskine to the charge. But the patron thought otherwise, and nominated Robert Stark to Kinross. The Presbytery declined to take action, but a Riding Committee carried through a farcical ordination and induction which was so resolutely opposed by the congregation that, by barring the Church building against the intrusionists, they forced them to carry through their work in other surroundings.

Erskine had all along been a strenuous opponent of patronage. "What difference," he once asked in the General Assembly, "does a piece of land make between man and man in the affairs of Christ's kingdom, which is not of this world? . . . We are told that 'God hath chosen the poor of this world, rich in faith'. It is not said that He hath chosen the heritors of this world, as we have done; but He hath chosen the poor of this world, rich in faith, and heirs of the kingdom. And if they be heirs of the kingdom, I wish to know by what warrant they are stripped of the privileges of the kingdom?"[3]

He later preached and published a sermon in which he declared "that those professed Presbyterians who thrust men upon congregations without the free choice their King had allowed them, were guilty of an attempt to jostle Christ out of His government, and to take it on their own shoulders."

The opposition of the patrons to Erskine is understandable in the light of such statements.

It was, however, his sermon as Moderator of the Synod of Perth and Stirling that brought him into his most serious collision with the Assembly. Insisting that "the call of the Church lies in the free choice and election of the Christian people," he went on to say that the promise of conduct and counsel in the choice of ministers "is not made to patrons, heritors, or any other set of men, but to the Church, the body of Christ, to whom apostles, prophets, evangelists, pastors and teachers are given."

And more in that strain.

Such plain speaking was more than the Assembly as then constituted was prepared to endure. Erskine's sermon was judged to be censurable, and, on his refusing to submit to rebuke, he was first suspended, and thereafter loosed from his charge. The three ministers who sided with him, James Fisher of Kinclaven, William Wilson of Perth, and Alexander Moncrieff of Abernethy, were similarly treated, and in December 1733 these four earnest and godly ministers constituted themselves into an associate Presbytery, thereby marking the first secession from the post-Revolution Church of Scotland.

More was to follow.

The operations of the Riding Committees were so obviously irregular that other means were resorted to for the purpose of intruding the unwanted ministers upon the congregations to which the patrons had presented them. The Assembly, secure in its Moderate majority, now passed legislation compelling Presbyteries to induct the patron's nominee, however strongly the congregations concerned might oppose them.

This tyrannical compulsion brought further disaster to the Church.

In 1751 a Mr Andrew Richardson was presented to the parish of Inverkeithing, but the Presbytery, on ascertaining the strong opposition of the people and their preference for another candidate, delayed proceeding with the induction of Mr Richardson. When this was reported to the Commission of Assembly in November of that year the Presbytery were ordered to induct Mr Richardson without delay under pain of "very high censure" in the event of disobedience. But when the Commission met again in March of the following year the unwanted minister was still not inducted. The case was left for final adjudication by the General Assembly in May. The Assembly ordered the Presbytery to meet at Inverkeithing on the approaching Thursday for the induction of the presentee. But when they met they were unable to muster the quorum of members stipulated by the Assembly and therefore could not proceed with the duty assigned them.

When they reported to the Assembly the following day six members of Presbytery gave in a "Humble Representation" in which they justified their non-compliance on the ground that the Act of 1736 forbade Presbyteries to intrude ministers upon parishes contrary to the will of the people. Others reported that they had gone to Inverkeithing, but, not finding the people present, had gone around the town trying to persuade them to assemble, but in vain. The remaining members who had met reported the reason for their inability to carry out the Presbytery's instruction.

The Assembly decided that one of the Dunfermline recusants should be deposed, and the lot fell upon Thomas Gillespie of Carnock, because he had gone further than the others in vindicating his non-compliance. An additional reason for the singling out of Gillespie, though it was not mentioned, was probably that he had attended at Perth some lectures delivered by a Professor adhering to the Secession, and that he had associated with Dissenters in England. Indeed, he had received ordination at the hands of the Independent, Dr Philip Doddridge, the hymn-writer. Gillespie was undoubtedly a man of warm piety whose character bore the impress of a sincere Christian experience. But Dean Stanley stands in little need of correction when he described him as "the latitudinarian, moderate, Christian-minded Gillespie". His easy-going ways were copied by his following and their inclusion in the United Presbyterian Church by the Union of 1847 did nothing to strengthen that Church in sound doctrine.

Gillespie afterwards preached in a meeting-house provided for him in Dunfermline. In 1761 he was joined by Thomas Boston of Oxnam (a son of the more famous Thomas Boston of Ettrick), and Thomas Colier of Colinsburgh. Together they formed a Presbytery of Relief "for the relief of Christians oppressed in their Christian privileges." Thereafter they were joined by many people who were becoming tired of the tyranny of the Church of Scotland.

Despite these secessions, the intrusion of ministers upon unwilling congregations continued, and unseemly incidents became frequent. In some cases the military were called in to assist in the enforcement of unpopular inductions. One of these was at Muckhart, where the intruder minister continued for 52 years, ministering to three or four hearers at services held in the dining-room of the manse, without communion services, and without a kirk-session. To turn his ample spare time to profitable account he leased a large farm and, in worldly reckoning, became a prosperous man.

Sometimes the local elders managed to outwit the patron, as in the case of the settlement of Dr Ronald Bayne in Kiltarlity. The local patron meeting with some of the elders one day, in an entirely different matter, remarked in conversation, "I suppose we shall have to take steps soon to fill the vacancy in the congregation. Was there any minister you had specially in mind in this connection?"

Well, they did have a minister "specially in mind," Ronald Bayne of Elgin, a man of somewhat fiery temperament, but a truly godly man and mighty in the Scriptures. But they well knew that to disclose the man of their choice to the patron would certainly mean that the presentation would go to another. So a quick-thinking elder replied with simulated servility, "O Sir, we would not be interfering with what is your privilege; but since you mention it, there is a rumour going that you were thinking of giving the presentation to Mr Bayne of Elgin. But surely, Sir, you would not be setting a crabbed man like that over us."

And that was precisely what happened, to the satisfaction of all parties, until the patron learned that he had been outwitted!

The Erskine and Gillespie secessions had taken away a large number of evangelical people from the Church, but there was still a considerable Evangelical party within the Church, and their work was being signally acknowledged and blessed by the Holy Spirit. Towards the close of the 18th century the effects of the Industrial Revolution, and even of the French Revolution, were clearly discernible in Scottish life. Democratic ideas entered deeply into social and industrial life and were matched by the ideals of ecclesiastical democracy proclaimed by the Covenanters, and by their successors in the Evangelical party of the post-Revolution Church. But alongside these developments, and of all-surpassing significance, was the fact that the whole country was experiencing the thrill of renewed spiritual life. John Willison testifies that "promising tokens began to appear of a revival of Christianity in 1740 and afterwards; for in Edinburgh and elsewhere some new praying societies were set up, and sundry students did associate with them, which gave hopes of a further reviving; and for this many prayers were put up through the land. . . ." The Associate

Presbytery brought George Whitefield to Scotland in 1741, and for three months he visited several populous centres preaching the reviving doctrines of grace with amazing results. Unhappily, the Seceders broke with him chiefly because he would not confine his preaching to their communion; but blessing continued to follow his labours. Some of the ministers who attended his meetings were awakened to a new sense of their spiritual need and of their pastoral responsibilities. The spirit of grace and of supplications was outpoured upon many congregations, and a new hunger for the Gospel manifested itself among the people. Evangelical ministers in the Highland parishes had experiences similar to those of their like-minded brethren in the South. Everywhere the Lord was confirming the Word with signs following.

To the Moderate party in the Church, the new evangelical enthusiasm was thoroughly distasteful, and the ministers principally associated with it were charged with vulgarising religion. Lay preaching in particular was frowned upon, and the General Assembly of 1799 sent out a pastoral letter warning the people against the Haldane brothers through whose teaching a strain of English Puritanism had entered into the religious life of Scotland.

Robert and James Haldane were of aristocratic connection, and were both converted in early life. Robert owned the estate of Airthrey, near Stirling, but sold it, with the intention of spending the proceeds on missionary work in India. Thwarted in this purpose by the East India Company, he and his brother turned their interest to Home Mission evangelism, for the need of such activity was only too evident. They had attended a parish church in the Island of Arran on a communion occasion, and were astonished when a general invitation was given to the congregation to come to the Lord's Table and met with no response. After a pause, James heard the sound of movement and, looking round, he saw the beadle with a long stick waking the people and poking them forward to the communion table.[3]

If any further evidence of the need for home evangelism was required it was supplied by the General Assembly's pastoral letter. The most unworthy motives were attributed to the Haldanes, and it was not surprising that the defamed men responded by denouncing the defective teaching of their accusers. Virtually extruded from the Church of Scotland, these gifted and godly men planned their activities along the lines of the Independency with which they had become familiar in England.

1. R. H. Story, *Life of William Carstares;* p. 328.
2. W. M. Hetherington, *History of the Church of Scotland;* p. 601.
3. J. Barr, *The United Free Church of Scotland;* p. 52.
4. Andrew Thomson, *Historical Sketch;* pp. 37, 129.
5. Allan Cameron, *Church of our Fathers;* p. 207.

CHAPTER EIGHT

THE EVANGELICAL REVIVAL

I looked up and saw what I never saw before—the fields already ripe unto harvest. I heard the Lord of the harvest commanding me to put in my sickle and reap.—James Robe of Kilsyth.

Despite the two secessions from the national Church, and the numerous desertions to Independency and Separatism, by the end of the 18th century there was a vigorous Evangelical party in the Church, and Moderate influence was visibly on the decline. The Evangelicals were under the powerful leadership of Dr John Erskine, whose intervention in the debate on Foreign Missions in the 1796 Assembly became historic. Hamilton of Gladsmuir, with the backing of Alexander ("Jupiter") Carlyle of Inveresk—both leading Moderates—had opposed a proposal that missionaries be sent to the heathen world, arguing that "men must be polished and refined in their manners before they can be properly enlightened in religious truths." "Where," asked Hamilton, "do we find the great Apostle of the Gentiles? Was it amongst barbarians, such as those to whom it was now proposed to carry the Gospel? Or was it not rather in the polished cities of Corinth, of Athens, and of Rome?"

It was then that Erskine rose to his feet and, pointing to the Bible, said, "Moderator, rax (reach) me that Bible." The portion that he chose to read from the Book was the account of Paul's shipwreck at Melita, in Acts 28. Reminding his audience that Paul had proclaimed himself a "debtor both to the Greeks and to the Barbarians; both to the wise and to the unwise," he added, "think you that when Paul wrought his miracles at Malta, and was taken to be a god, he did not also preach Christ to the barbarians, and explain whose name it was through which such power was given unto men?"

This rather dramatic intervention had the effect of silencing the advocates of a Christianity that bypassed the barbarians and offered its benefits only to the civilised and cultured world, but not, as yet, of securing a majority in the Assembly for the work of foreign missions. For that result the Evangelicals had yet to wait awhile.

Dr Erskine was succeeded in the Evangelical primacy by the celebrated Dr Andrew Thomson, of St George's Church,

Edinburgh. Popular preacher though he was, Thomson probably made his fullest contribution to the Church's struggle for spiritual independence through the trenchant articles which appeared in his *Christian Instructor* from time to time. But Dr Thomson was cut off at the height of his usefulness, and was succeeded in the leadership of his party by Dr Thomas Chalmers. Chalmers, who had begun his ministry as a Moderate—although as one of the best specimens of that school—had undergone a sound conversion, and now was among the most powerful protagonists of Evangelicalism in the whole Assembly.

During this period church extension work was prosecuted with vigour, and new pastoral charges were springing up, especially in the rapidly developing urban areas. Provision had been made at the time of the Union of the Parliaments for the erection of new churches in these areas, but the heritors had so much say in the matter that church extension did not keep pace with the needs of the people. This led to the building of churches by voluntary contributions, and Chapels of Ease, as these were called, gathered to them large numbers of the people. The impetus for this work came mainly from the Evangelical Party, and it was opposed by the Moderates; for the support of these new congregations would naturally go to the party to which they owed their existence. Up to 1834 the ministers of these Chapels of Ease were under certain disabilities. They had liberty to preach, but were excluded from all the courts of the Church, and it was only after a long struggle that they were eventually given parity with their brethren in the parish churches.

A growing sense of responsibility for the unattached masses at home was now matched by an increasing zeal for the evangelisation of the heathen abroad. Nor were the claims of the Jews overlooked, and in 1838 Robert Murray McCheyne of Dundee, with Dr Alexander Black of Aberdeen and Dr Alexander Keith, of St Cyrus, visited Palestine in the interests of Jewish Missions. The revived spirit of the Church was revealing itself in all the departments of her work. Her prolonged tribulation had the effect of deepening the prayer-life of her believing people as they earnestly cried for Divine help. In times of spiritual deadness questions relating to doctrine and Church government are apt to be reckoned as of little account; but it is a sign of the activity of the Holy Spirit among the Lord's people when there is a sensitiveness to Christ's claims and a desire to regulate the affairs of His Kingdom according to the teaching of His Word.

Under the inspiring leadership of Dr Chalmers the pressure for reform was maintained in the General Assembly. The old law which required that the minister to be settled in a parish must have a call from the people had been ignored, but never repealed, and a resolute effort was now made on what came to be known as the Veto Plan to make it effective. In 1833 Dr Chalmers had introduced a motion proposing that "the dissent of a majority of the male heads of families, resident within the parish, being members of the congregation and in communion with the Church, at least two years previous to the day of moderation (of the call), whether such dissent be expressed with or without the assignment of reasons, ought to be of conclusive effect in setting aside the presentee (under the patron's nomination), save and except where it is clearly established by the patron, presentee, or any of the minority, that the said dissent is founded in corrupt and malicious combination, or not truly founded on any objection personal to the presentee in regard to his ministerial gifts and qualifications, either in general, or with reference to that particular parish."

Chalmers showed the evil of the patronage system in the respect that the patron might be "an infidel or an atheist, a fool or a knave, a scoundrel to society and a foe to godliness; but because he had bought, or inherited, a certain civil right, he has the chief power in the selection of the man who is to minister in holy things to a Christian congregation."

The motion was lost by the narrow margin of twelve votes, but when a similar motion was submitted in the following year—this time by Lord Moncreiff—Dr Chalmers not being a member of Assembly—it was carried by a majority of forty-six, and thereby the long reign of Moderatism in the General Assembly was ended.

Opposition to the Veto Act has sometimes been grounded on its vulnerability to abuse. Factions in congregations, it has been alleged, could bring it into operation maliciously to bring about the rejection of a thoroughly worthy and competent minister. But this is to overlook the fact that the sustaining of a call to a minister was the function of the local Presbytery who, prior to this action, would require to judge as to the validity of any objections that might be made against the proposed settlement. In point of fact, the Veto was not often used. It is judged that in the five years preceding the Disruption, out of 150 ministerial settlements, 140 were harmonious.

The Veto Plan was challenged almost from the moment of its passing. In October 1834, a licentiate of the Church, Robert Young, was presented to the parish of Auchterarder in Perthshire. But when it came to the signing of the call only three persons signified their concurrence in the patron's choice, while 287 recorded their veto against him. On appeal to the General Assembly, that court, acting in accordance with the Veto plan instructed the Presbytery to reject Young. This decision was immediately opposed by the patron and his nominee who raised an action in the Court of Session asking for a declaration that the General Assembly had exceeded its powers in passing the Veto Act. The decision went in favour of Young and his patron, the Earl of Kinnoull. This was a reversion to the old Stewart doctrine that the Church must obey the State in all matters of dispute. "That our Saviour," said the Lord President of the Court, "is the Head of the Kirk of Scotland in any temporal, or legislative, or judicial sense, is a position which I can dignify by no other name than absurdity. The Parliament is the temporal head of the Church, from whose Acts, and from whose Acts alone, it exists as a National Church, and from which alone it derives all its powers."[1]

This decision was a flat contradiction of Andrew Melville's assertion of the co-ordinate jurisdiction of Church and State, and it marked the beginning of a new phase in the Church's struggle for spiritual independence. Hitherto, all the acts of intrusion upon unwilling and protesting congregations had been perpetrated by a party within the Church itself, with the assistance of the civil courts when applied for. Now the rights and privileges of the Church were to be taken into custody by the State, and the law of the land was declared to be that a man, duly qualified educationally and morally, and securing the presentation of the patron, must be inducted to the charge in question, whether or not he was acceptable to the congregation.

Inevitably, this revolutionary ruling caused chaos and confusion throughout the Church. Intrusions became more frequent, and in cases where patrons had second thoughts about their presentees and tried to meet the people's desire by making an alternative nomination, the Court of Session would not allow it. In another parish in Perthshire itself, for example, where the presentee sought to break open the church door and force his way into the pulpit in defiance of the people, the patron had the good sense to withdraw his presentation and give it to another man who was acceptable to the congregation. But the Court of Session forbade the ordination of the second man, and when the Presbytery disregarded their ban, they were rebuked at the bar of the civil court and narrowly (by one vote) escaped imprisonment. The fines laid upon them were so heavy as to be well-nigh ruinous, as they were probably meant to be; but friends stepped in and contributed to the help of the faithful ministers who had proved themselves ready to face any hardship that might come rather than break their ordination vows by which they had pledged their loyalty and obedience to Christ and His Church.

There were several other outrageous invasions of the Church's province by the civil courts, but the one that achieved the greatest notoriety of all, and that made the disruption inevitable, was the intrusion at Marnoch, in the Presbytery of Strathbogie. The presentation in this case had gone to John Edwards, a local schoolmaster who had been part-time assistant to the recently deceased Mr William Stronach, who had been minister at Marnoch for over 30 years. A more unfortunate presentation could scarcely have been made; for Edwards, on the representation of the parishioners, had been removed from his assistantship about a year before the death of Mr Stronach! When, therefore, the call was produced, only one parishioner signed it—Peter Taylor, a local innkeeper, while 261 male heads of families signed the Veto against him.

In the circumstances, the trustees of the patron revoked the presentation to Edwards and extended it to David Henry, who had succeeded Edwards as assistant and was thoroughly acceptable to the people. But Edwards invoked the Court of Session decision with regard to Auchterarder, and the Presbytery were instructed to take him on trials for ordination. The Moderates had a majority in the Presbytery and were ready to act on the order of the Court of Session. The Commission of Assembly intervened and forbade the ordination. The seven ministers who indicated their intention of proceeding with the ordination despite the Commission's ban, were then suspended and so deprived of their power to ordain. The seven nevertheless proceeded to act on the instruction of the civil court. On a snowy day in January 1841 they met at Marnoch where a crowded congregation awaited them. But the purpose of the parishioners in gathering was not to welcome the new minister but to hand in a formal protest, together with the warning that if it were disregarded they would leave in a body. Disregarded it was; and, true to their intention, the congregation left the church, taking their Bibles with them, never to return. John Edwards was ordained and inducted—to use Dr W. G. Blaikie's words, "as nominally minister of Marnoch, but really minister of Peter Taylor."[2] Dr William Hanna has described the event as "an ordination altogether unparalleled in the history of the Church, performed by a presbytery of suspended ministers, on the call of a single communicant, against the desire of the patron, in face of the strenuous opposition of a united congregation, in opposition to the express injunction of the Assembly, and at the sole bidding, and under the sole authority of the Court of Session."

The Assembly, in the exercise of its disciplinary powers, deposed the seven refractory ministers, but the Court of Session reacted by suspending the sentence of deposition and interdicting the other ministers of the Church from preaching in the Strathbogie church buildings without their consent. And when the Church sent ministers to preach elsewhere in Strathbogie than in the church buildings from which they were banned, the Court of Session, by a majority, granted an extended interdict forbidding them to preach anywhere in the district, whether indoors or out.

Dr Thomas Guthrie, of Edinburgh, tells how he treated the extended interdict. "In going to preach at Strathbogie," he writes, "I was met by an interdict from the Court of Session—an interdict to which, as regards civil matters, I gave implicit obedience. On the Lord's Day, when I was preparing for Divine service, in came a servant of the law and handed me an interdict. I told him he had done his duty and I would do mine. The interdict forbade me, under penalty of the Calton Hill Jail, to preach the Gospel in the parish churches of Strathbogie. I said, the parish churches are stone and lime and belong to the State; I will not intrude there. It forbade me to preach the Gospel in the schoolhouses. I said, the schoolhouses are stone and lime and belong to the State; I will not intrude there. It forbade me to preach in the churchyard, and I said, the dust of the dead is the State's, and I will not intrude there. But when these Lords of the Session forbade me to preach my Master's blessed Gospel and offer salvation to sinners anywhere in that district under the arch of heaven, I put the interdict under my feet, and I preached the Gospel."[3]

Events in Marnoch had the effect of bringing to the notice of the whole country the complete impasse which now existed between the Church and the civil courts. Bit by bit the Court of Session had built up its control over the Church, withdrawing the right of congregations to choose their own pastors, nullifying the Church's discipline in her own courts, over-ruling her legislation, interdicting commissioners from the Presbytery of Strathbogie from taking their seats in the General Assembly, and even interfering with the operation of patronage itself when the patron accepted the people's rejection of his nominee and made an alternative presentation. The fact that the bi-centenary of the famous Covenanting Assembly of 1638 fell in this period of acute ecclesiastical controversy had its own effect in heightening interest in the Church's struggle for the retention of her spiritual independence, the surrender of which would be regarded as a betrayal of the cause for which the Covenanters had suffered persecution, imprisonment and even death.

A clear hint of coming events was given at the General Assembly of 1842, when Major Ludovic Stewart drew attention to the interdict served on him. "Moderator," he said, "I hold in my hand a document which has been sent to me within the last few days. It is an interdict from the Court of Session prohibiting me from taking my seat in the Assembly as the elder from the Presbytery of Strathbogie. I am not one of those who treat lightly an interdict of a civil court, for I have long been accustomed to strict discipline. But I hold that there are circumstances in which an individual may be placed when it would be criminal to obey the interdict of any earthly Court. I hold in my hand an authority in this holy book (his Bible) which does not prohibit me from standing forth in support of the principles of the Church of Scotland in which I have been brought up, and, so long as I am permitted, I will serve God as faithfully as I have served my country—and I am ready to serve my country again, whenever the time arrives and the circumstances may come when I may be called upon to do so."[4]

The soldier from Strathbogie voiced the prevailing mood of the Assembly. The interdicted commissioners were asked to take their seats, and the Assembly minuted a strong protest against "the attempt now for the first time made on the part of any civil tribunal to interfere with the constitution of the Supreme Court of this Church." Furthermore, the Assembly addressed to the Government its *Claim, Declaration and Protest* in objection to the State's high-handed invasion upon the province of the Church.

"By that solemn instrument," writes Dr Robert Buchanan, with reference to the *Claim,* "the Church took all men to witness that there was now but one or other of two alternatives open to her—either to get her Claim acknowledged and allowed by the Legislature, or to abandon her civil establishment."[5]

The *Claim* is a well-reasoned document. Beginning with a statement of what the Church of Scotland regarded as the doctrines and principles essential to her continuance as an established Church, viz. the sole Headship of Jesus Christ and the government of the Church in the hands of office-bearers distinct from the Civil Magistrate, it proceeds to cite the authoritative laws and standards of the Church in support of these positions, and the statutes of the realm in recognition of them. It shows that in spite of these guaranteed rights, the Church has been invaded by the secular tribunal in several points of jurisdiction, as, for example:—

(1) By interdicting Presbyteries of the Church from admitting to a pastoral charge, as had been done at Stewarton, even although the Presbytery made no claim on the civil benefice.

(2) By ordering a Church court, as in the case of the Presbytery of Strathbogie, to take a licentiate on trial for ordination, and induct him to Marnoch, against the will of the people.

(3) By prohibiting the communicants from intimating their dissent from a call to be given to a minister, as at Daviot.

(4) By interdicting the preaching of the Gospel throughout a whole district by any minister of the Church under authority of

the Church courts, as at Strathbogie, thus arrogating to the civil court the jurisdiction of the Church.

(5) By holding members of Presbyteries liable to damages for obeying the laws of the General Assembly to which they had vowed to give obedience.

(6) By interdicting the General Assembly from inflicting church censures as when interdict was granted against a sentence of deposition against a minister found guilty of theft.

(7) By interdicting members of the General Assembly from taking their seats in the same, as in the case of the Strathbogie commissioners.

All this, it was pointed out, had been done in opposition to God's Word; the Confession of Faith ratified by statute; in breach of the Treaty of Union; and contrary to divers Acts of Legislature.

The *Claim* leaves no doubt as to what result all this was to have for the Church unless the grievances complained of were amended; for it warns that inasmuch as other encroachments were threatened, and the government and discipline of the Church could not be carried out under such conditions, the Church while valuing, as she had always done, the benefits of State connection, must, even at the risk of the loss of these, "persevere in maintaining her liberties as a Church of Christ, and in carrying on the government thereof on her own constitutional principles, and must refuse to intrude ministers on her congregations, to obey the unlawful coercion attempted to be enforced against her in the exercise of her spiritual functions and jurisdiction, or to consent that her people be deprived of their rightful liberties."

This famous manifesto concluded by protesting that all the Acts of Parliament of Great Britain passed without the consent of the Church and Nation in derogation of the rights and privileges of the Church were null and void; as were also all sentences of courts in contravention of the rights and privileges of the Church. And they declare that "it shall be free to the members of this Church, or their successors, at any time hereafter, when there shall be a prospect of obtaining justice, to claim the restitution of all such civil rights and privileges, and temporal benefits and endowments, as for the present they may be compelled to yield up, in order to preserve to their office-bearers the free exercise of their spiritual government and discipline, and to their people the liberties, of which respectively it had been attempted, so contrary to law and justice, to deprive them."[6]

In submitting her *Claim*, however, the Church gave her implicit pledge that she would submit to the civil courts in civil matters, as she had always done, and would always give due respect to the jurisdiction of the secular tribunal, but she insisted that this tribunal had no power to review the sentence of church courts in spiritual matters, or to "coerce them in the exercise of such jurisdiction."

The government made the tragic mistake of treating the representations of the aggrieved Church with lofty disdain. The opposition of the legislature had been stiffened by the Church's disregard of the judgments given—an attitude which Lord Cockburn, one of the Scottish judges, found indefensible. Crediting the judges who had opposed the Church's claims with having given what they honestly believed to be the law, he considers that they felt provoked by the Church's resistance to their judgments; "but a Court," he adds, "has no right to be provoked."

The suspicion lingers, however, that personal prejudices were reflected in the attitude of some of the Church's most influential opponents. Lord Melbourne, the Prime Minister during part of that period of crisis, was known to have no love for reformers or dissenters. For Dr Chalmers, the leader of the Non-Intrusionists, he had the heartiest dislike. Sir James Graham, the Home Secretary, who was responsible also for Scottish affairs, was fixed in the idea that the situation in Scotland needed the strong hand of the State. John Hope, Dean of the Faculty of Advocates, and afterwards Lord-Justice Clerk, was a dyed-in-the-wool Moderate and the counsellor of that party in all their moves against the Evangelicals.*

In November 1842 the Evangelicals held a Convocation in Roxburgh Church, Edinburgh, to plan for the breach with the State which now appeared inevitable. There was an attendance of over 470 ministers in St George's Church for the pre-Convocation service, where Dr Thomas Chalmers preached a memorable sermon on the words, "Unto the upright there ariseth light in the darkness," (Psalm 112: 4). The preacher's message related to the solemn business which had brought them together. "Frankly, and without disguise," writes Dr Thomas Brown, "he pointed to the darkness gathering round the Church's path of duty, and then broke forth in the confidence of assured faith as he spoke of the light promised to the upright." The great lesson that he found in the text was "the connection which obtains between integrity of

*As an instance of Hope's strong bias, Dr W. G. Blaikie tells, in his *After Fifty Years*, that in the autumn after the Disruption, Hope was presiding at a justiciary trial at Aberdeen, in the course of which a certificate of character relating to the accused man was read. The certificate was signed, on behalf of the Kirk Session of Drumblade Free Church, by Dr Blaikie who, at the time, was minister of Drumblade Free Church. Lord Hope was indignant at the submission of the certificate, and railed at "the arrogance of these people," declaring that the law knew but one Kirk Session in the parish, and could hear nothing from any other. "The best of the joke," comments Dr Blaikie, "was that in the church by law established in that parish there was then neither minister, nor elder, nor session-clerk, nor kirk-officer, nor any single vestige of what a kirk-session should be."

purpose and clearness of perception." Perplexities as to the path of duty was often the experience of the Church of Jesus Christ and of the individual believer. But when these perplexities were faced conscientiously and in submission to Divine guidance, the needed enlightenment would not be withheld. "Ye men of God," cried the preacher, "who make the Bible the supreme directory of your hearts and consciences, you will not long be left in uncertainty. He will make your way clear and open before you. If before Him we come with the docility of little children, He will cause us in understanding to be men."

It was in this mood of humble submission to the guidance of God's Word and Spirit that the Convocation began its work and carried through its programme. There were frequent sessions for prayer, and the sermon preached by Chalmers proved to be prophetic. Many of those present testified to the enlightenment that had come to them as to their duty and the way of going about it, as the discussions continued. The experience of Dr Chalmers in his Church Extension work proved most valuable in the planning which had to be carried through for the maintenance of the unendowed Church which would emerge from the Disruption if the Church's last appeal to the Government failed. His Sustentation Fund plan for the maintenance of the ministry and the supply of Gospel ordinances was accepted by the gathering. It was resolved that a special effort be made to keep the people informed of the matters in dispute and of the decision to put their rights and liberties in the forefront of their contendings. Hugh Miller had already done excellent work in this connection through the medium of *The Witness,* and the Church's case was argued from both sides through the many pamphlets that were sent into circulation. The very fact that so many eminent ministers of the Church were prepared to sign away their homes and means of livelihood, and go into the wilderness, impressed the people with the gravity of the questions at issue and made Church affairs the topic of discussion all over the country and at all levels of society.

The importance of the Convocation as a preparation for the Disruption which was now regarded as unavoidable cannot be over-stressed. It gave cohesion to the Evangelicals; it clarified the situation for brethren ill-formed and uncertain; it provided a plan whereby the work of the Church of Scotland could still be carried on by a body of men pledged to the old standards and yet free from interference by a dominating legislature in the exercise of powers conferred upon her by her heavenly King, and guaranteed to her, not only by successive Acts of Parliament, but also in the Coronation Oath of the temporal Sovereign. The Convocation was so evidently the crossing of the Rubicon that Dr W. G. Blaikie writes, "We had all now to busy ourselves with preparation for the Disruption".[7]

The Memorial sent to the Government by the Convocation failed of its purpose, as the signatories themselves had expected. It was rejected by a majority of 241 to 76. Parliament refused even to appoint a Committee of Enquiry into the Church's case; but it is worthy of note that the Scottish members in the proportion of more than two to one, supported the motion.

It was a fateful decision. Robert Murray McCheyne, the saintly young minister of St Peter's, Dundee, who had attended all diets of the Convocation but did not survive to take his intended part in the Disruption, wrote of that session of Parliament. "An eventful night this in the British Parliament. Once more King Jesus stands at an earthly tribunal, *and they know Him not.*"[7]

The thoroughness of the planning carried through by the ministers who had attended the Convocation in November 1842 meant that the work of the first Free Church of Scotland General Assembly in May of the following year was transacted with quiet efficiency. The sermon preached by Dr Welsh at the opening service of the undivided General Assembly of the Church of Scotland was an appeal to the sober judgment of his audience rather than to their emotions earlier in the day. His text was, "Let every man be fully persuaded in his own mind" (Roms. xiv: 5), and some writers have taken his choice of theme as an indication that he was himself a victim of uncertainty; but his sermon gives a very different impression. It was the utterance of a man who, having made up his own mind, desired that his hearers should make conscience of the decision of the day as he himself had already done. Stressing the necessity of Bible-grounded convictions in so serious a matter, he urged that "it is not enough that they conceive that another constitution is more desirable, or that they believe it to be secured to them by the ancient constitution of their country, or that it is in conformity with the opinions of the fathers of the Reformation, and the original standards of the Church. Such views may strengthen their abstract convictions as theologians, or they may affect their ideas of their rights as citizens; but unless they believe their principles to have such sanction from Scripture as to render it sinful for them to surrender them, the guilt of schism would be incurred in separating from the Church of their fathers. But if they are fully persuaded that their course is the only one that is warranted by the Word of God, they are not to have a stumbling-block put before them."

1. P. Bayne, *The Free Church of Scotland;* p. 102.
2. W. G. Blaikie, *After Fifty Years;* p. 22.

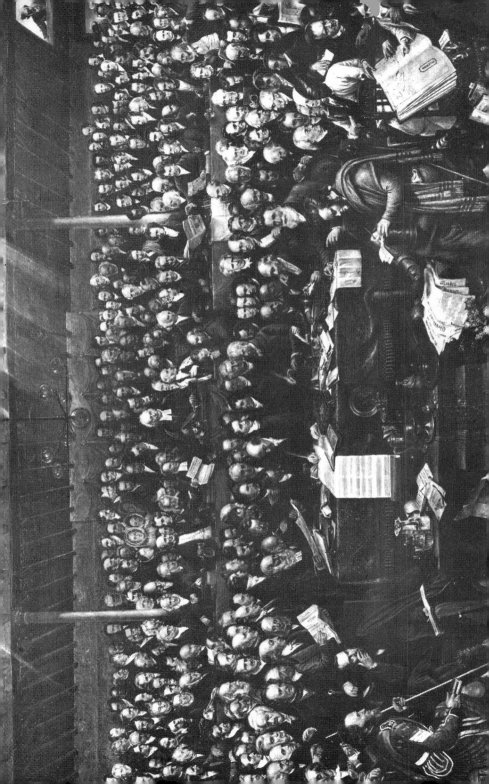

The Floating Church, Strontian (see page 66)

The Free Church Communion Service, Ferintosh, September 1843

Preceding page: *Signing the Deed of Demission: Tanfield Hall, May 1843* (see page 61)

3. D. K. and C. J. Guthrie, *Life of Thomas Guthrie;* vol. 1, p. 18.
4. D. A. Mackinnon, *Some Chapters in Scottish Church History;* pp. 178, 179.
5. ibid. p. 179.
6. *Authorised Standards of the Free Church.*
7. Thomas Brown, *Annals of the Disruption;* p. 76.

E

CHAPTER NINE

THE CHURCH OF SCOTLAND, FREE

I can conceive nothing nobler than the position which our Church occupied when she presented her Claim of Rights to the Government of this country, and at the same time expressed a resolution to receive no emoluments as the price of her liberty to serve Christ alone.—*Dr John Kennedy of Dingwall.*

To the last the opponents of the Evangelicals refused to take the threat of disruption seriously. If indeed a break did take place, the outgoing ministers would be a negligible minority, and the chilling winds of poverty would soon cool their hot heads and send them back in more tractable spirit. Dr Elder Cumming of London, well known for his interest in unfulfilled prophecy, ventured the confident prediction that of the large number who had pledged themselves to separation in the event of their failure to secure recognition of the Church's *Claim of Rights*, "more than three-fourths, probably the whole" would go back on their word. Others limited their estimate of the outgoing ministers to forty, and Mr Murray Dunlop, M.P. for Greenock, whose clear brain had conceived the *Claim, Declaration and Protest*, tells us that even within a few hours of the Disruption the discussions between the Lord High Commissioner and his guests at Holyrood Palace produced the calculation that "the number who would separate would be between twenty and thirty."

The wishful thinking of the Moderates committed them to estimates that later embarrassed them. Dr Alexander Beith of Stirling records that one of them "engaged to put all the ministers who should come out into a hat."[1] Another of the same party volunteered to "eat them." Lord Justice Clerk Hope, in a moment of prophetic inspiration, guaranteed that the result of the Disruption would be "most inconsiderable." There were not six or ten ministers who would secede. "Within a year of the event," he affirmed, "people will wonder at the anxiety they first felt, and will laugh at the secession and its wooden churches." The foolish prognostications of John Hope did much to determine the attitude of Sir James Graham, the Scottish Secretary, towards the Non-Intrusionists — an attitude which, later, he deeply regretted; for, writing eleven years after the Disruption, he says, "I have never ceased to regret that occurrence; and when I look at its consequences I take great blame to myself and have a painful misgiving that more might have been done by me to avert so great a calamity."

With so many conflicting estimates in currency it is not surprising that the crowds outside St Andrew's Church on that fateful day in May 1843 were still in doubt as to what might happen. Suddenly, however, those nearest the doors raised the excited cry, "They come! They come!" and the familiar figures of Dr David Welsh, Dr Thomas Chalmers and Dr Robert Gordon were seen emerging, closely followed by such notables as Dr Patrick Macfarlan of Greenock, Dr Thomas Brown of Glasgow, and Dr John MacDonald of Ferintosh. Row upon row they came, until over 400 ministers had left the building, with a large number of ruling-elder Commissioners. The sight stirred even the phlegmatic citizens of Edinburgh. Cheer upon cheer rang through the thronged streets, and the less demonstrative of the bystanders greeted the passing churchmen with such words as "The Lord be with you," and "God guide you." Lord Jeffrey of the Court of Session, on hearing of what had happened, threw all judicial restraint to the winds in his excitement and cried, as he tossed aside the book he had been reading, "I am proud of my country. There is not another country upon earth where such a deed could have been done."[2]

Tanfield Hall was packed to the doors when Dr Welsh opened the proceedings and constituted the Assembly. Under the practised Moderatorship of Dr Chalmers, (for he had been Moderator of the General Assembly in 1832), the first General Assembly of the Free Church of Scotland proceeded to its work. A Provisional Committee which had been set up in Edinburgh a few days earlier so as to prepare for the day of decision had done its work so effectively that confusion was largely eliminated. The Committee had operated in three sections taking charge respectively of finance, architecture and statistics. The usual committees were appointed to expedite the business of the court, and the Assembly faced up to the tremendous task of reorganisation with which it was now confronted.

At the evening meeting of the opening day Dr Robert Buchanan drew attention to the unusual wording of the Queen's letter to the undivided General Assembly. It contained the following paragraph: "It behoves you to remember that unity in the Church is the bond of peace, but that schism and its pernicious effects may tend seriously to endanger that religious Establishment from which Scotland has derived inestimable benefits." The letter reminded the Assembly that "the rights and properties of an Established Church are conferred by law; it is by law that the Church of Scotland is united with the State, and that her endowments are secured; and the ministers of religion, claiming the sanction of law in defence of their privileges, are specially bound, by their sacred calling, to be examples of obedience."[3]

The undertones of the letter were resented by the Non-Intrusionists, and the reference to the dangers of schism evoked a spirited retort from Dr Buchanan. Unity in the Church, he said, "is not that which constitutes the bond of peace. The bond of peace can only be constituted by the Spirit of God enlightening the minds and sanctifying the hearts of men with God's truth. There can be no unity but a unity of the truth as it is in Jesus. . . . As was stated by the venerable McCrie, 'Schism and separation are not identical.' There may be separations which are made, not to break, but to preserve the unity of the Spirit of God; and I solemnly believe that the separation which we have now made is a separation of this kind. What have we separated from? We have not separated from the Word of God, which we regard as the only infallible rule of faith and manners. We do not separate from the *Confession of Faith*, which we do truthfully and assuredly regard as the sound and Scriptural exposition of the Word of God. We do not separate from the standards of the Church's policy, which we venerate as founded on and agreeable to God's holy Word . . . God's Word is lying before our Moderator. The ancient laws and constitution of the Church of Scotland are here entire. We have separated from none of these. But we have separated from the civil power — separated, because, while connected with it, we could no longer maintain our position except at the expense of trampling under foot what we regard as the immutable principles of truth."[4]

There was a warm response from the Assembly as Buchanan, with vigour and vehemence, repudiated the conception of the Church as the creature of the State, as so clearly implied in the Queen's letter.

The *Deed of Demission*, by which the protesting ministers separated themselves from the Establishment, was submitted to the Assembly on Tuesday, May 23rd. Twice it was read over to a hushed audience and then adopted, not by general acclamation, but by "the expressive votes of ministers." The signatories came forward in groups of ten, and arrangements were made whereby ministers who were not present at that Assembly might have the opportunity of adhibiting their names later.

The famous picture, by D. O. Hill, R.S.A., of the signing of the Deed is a worthy memorial of a great occasion. Hill, a Free Churchman himself, had been an eye-witness of events in the Tanfield Hall, and had been encouraged by Dr Robert Buchanan and Lord Cockburn of the Court of Session to devote his talent to the production of a memorial of this kind, Cockburn remarking that "since the days of Knox (if even in Knox's days) there had never been an event so well worthy of being transmitted to posterity by the artist's hands."

For over twenty years Mr Hill laboured at his chosen task, producing in the end a canvas that was highly praised by Sir George Harvey, President of the Scottish Academy, who said, "The painting is unique of its kind; I know nothing like it existing."

Much thought was given to the lay-out of the picture, for Hill decided that it should be of a widely representative character. Town and Gown are represented by Sir James Forrest and Sir David Brewster, Lord Provost of Edinburgh and Principal of Edinburgh University respectively, and both ardent Free Churchmen. The Law is represented by the inclusion of several leading members of the Bench and Bar, and the nobility by the presence of such men of distinction as the Marquis of Breadalbane, the Hon. Fox Maule (afterwards Earl of Dalhousie), Sir Andrew Agnew of Lochawe, and Sir Thomas MacDougall Brisbane, President of the Royal Society — all of whom, each in his own way, had been loyal helpers of the Church in her time of crisis. The friendship of other Churches at home and abroad is acknowledged by the prominence given to their delegates in the group, and deserved distinction is accorded to many ladies who had helped outstandingly with the maintaining of the Evangelical testimony. The central figures, of course, are the Moderator and Clerks of Assembly. At the Clerk's table, in the act of signing the *Deed of Demission*, is Dr Patrick Macfarlan of Greenock, who signed away the richest living of all. Awaiting his turn to sign is Dr John MacDonald, of Ferintosh, perhaps the best known of the group around him. Standing at a pillar high above the table, is to be seen Dr R. S. Candlish, with the Roll of Assembly in hand, as he calls forward the groups to sign. And at the right-hand end of the table it is easy to pick out such figures as Dr Alexander Duff and Dr John Duncan, representative of Foreign and Jewish Missions. Neither man in fact was present in the Assembly that day to sign the Deed, but even at the expense of a touch of anachronism the artist included them in symbol of the Church's interest in the regions beyond, and in acknowledgment of the enthusiastic support given by almost all the missionaries to the Free Church of Scotland.

In the foreground of the picture are to be seen the figures of Sergeant Mackenzie, a Waterloo veteran, who acted as Assembly Officer; Thomas L. Hately, the Assembly Precentor; and Hugh Miller, the geologist who, as editor of *The Witness*, did so much to instruct the people in the matters at issue.

The picture may be seen in the Free Church Presbytery Hall, in Edinburgh.

Sir George Harvey, whose comment on the Assembly picture is

quoted above, made his own contribution to the artistic memorials of the Disruption in his well-known and widely-copied picture *Leaving the Manse*, of which Dr Chalmers remarked, "It will do more for our cause than a hundred of our pamphlets." The minister in the picture was compounded by Harvey of Dr John Bruce's picturesque head and Dr Thomas Guthrie's stately figure. The minister lends the support of his arm to his aged mother, while his wife locks the door of the Manse for the last time and leads her young family away from their old home. It is a picture that brings home to the viewer in a forcible way the involvement of young and old, weak and strong, in the sacrifices which the maintenance of the Church's spiritual freedom demanded.

The silversmiths also provided memorials of the 1843 Free Church Assembly, principally in the shape of a commemorative medallion and a brooch. The latter in particular is a fascinating piece of symbolism. The outer wreath of thistles symbolises Scotland, and the Burning Bush in the centre is the familiar emblem of the Scottish Church. The cluster of tombstones, bearing the names of the principal Reformers, the four dates, 1560, 1592, 1638 and 1843, and the addition of the names of Chalmers, Dunlop and Candlish, together with the 86 word comment engraved on the back of the brooch, present the claim of the Free Church of Scotland to be in lineal and loyal descent from the Reformed Church of 1560.

For a time there appeared to be some indecision as to the name which the new denomination was to assume. The Disruption leaders were well aware that no body of Christians in the country had a better right than they, and the church which they led, to be designated the Church of Scotland, for they were the true defenders of the historic constitution and establishment of that Church. "We meet not at this time," said Dr Thomas Brown, in his Moderatorial address to the second General Assembly of the Free Church of Scotland, held at Glasgow in October of Disruption year, "for the purpose of framing a new Constitution for the Church of Scotland. That Constitution, under the guidance of the Spirit of God, has been framed by the skill and the wisdom of our forefathers — men of eminence, and the men of God of former times — our Protestant Reformers; and it existed before it was brought into connection with the State at all. By that Constitution we abide steadfastly. Our Standards, our Books of Discipline, our Creed, our Confession of Faith, we retain in all their original integrity. To them we have adhered; to them we have appealed; by them we have sought to be tested in all our recent contendings; but we were derided as men of extravagant views, of presumptuous ideas. We therefore, this being the case, maintain that we are the Church of Scotland."[5]

Dr R. S. Candlish made a similar claim when, in 1856, he declared, "The date of the existence of the present Established Church of Scotland is 1843; the date of *our* existence is 1560."

While holding this view, however, the Disruption leaders were well aware that their assumption of the old designation would immediately be disallowed in the Law Courts. An alternative designation, still embodying their claim, would therefore have to be found. In the early meetings of their Assembly they were wont to refer to themselves as the Free Protesting Church of Scotland, and, sometimes, as the Free Presbyterian Church of Scotland, but both names were soon dropped. The only point of distinction to be stressed between the new body and that from which it separated in consequence of the Disruption was that the Church represented by the gatherings in the Tanfield Hall was Free — free from the oppressive and unscriptural domination of what Chalmers had called a "vitiated Establishment." Their ultimate choice of title therefore was the *Church of Scotland-Free*; or, in the form which soon gained preference, the *Free Church of Scotland.**

The volume of business, and the rapidly developing organisation of the Free Church, necessitated the holding of a second General Assembly in 1843. Plans for the pastoral care of the people were made. The building of churches, manses and schools proved a vast undertaking. Furthermore, colleges had to be provided for the training of ministers and teachers, and the needs of the mission fields had to be assessed and provided against. Altogether it was a year of ceaseless activity.

*The choice of name, apparently, was finalised by Dr Chalmers. Principal Rainy brought in a reference to it in his Assembly speech on the Union overture in 1900. He remembered very well, he said, in his father's drawing room, when he was a lad, his mother saying to Dr Chalmers, "Dr Chalmers, who was it that fixed upon that excellent name for our church?" and he remembered Dr Chalmers saying, "Well, madam, I rather think I had something to do with it."

1. Alexander Beith, *Memories of Disruption Times;* p. 26.
2. Thomas Brown, *Annals of the Disruption;* p. 95.
3. *Proceedings of Free Church General Assembly;* May 1843; p. 23.
4. ibid. pp. 26, 27.
5. *Proceedings of Free Church General Assembly;* Oct. 1843, pp. 2, 3.

CHAPTER TEN

REBUILDING THE WALLS

*All were now as busy building as before in battling for
our freedom, that we might again raise our heads as a
Church in the land.—Rev. George Lewis of Dundee.*

Meanwhile, what had happened in the residuary Assembly
which had continued its sessions in St Andrew's Church?

Their first concern was to replace the Retiring Moderator, Dr
Welsh, who was now in the Free Church of Scotland. Principal
Haldane of St Andrews, as the oldest ex-Moderator present, was
called to the Chair to open proceedings. Thereafter, Principal
Macfarlane of Glasgow University was elected Moderator.

The document which Dr Welsh had left on the table before
departing called for action, but the Assembly seemed rather
uncertain as to what to do with it. Eventually it was agreed that it
be remitted to a Committee for consideration and report. But the
claims made in the *Protest* were difficult to refute and impossible
to brush aside; with the result that to this day they remain
unanswered.

With the Moderates once more in power the General Assembly
proceeded to get rid of all the legislation which had been carried
against them in the preceding nine years, and the recalcitrant
Strathbogie ministers were treated as if they had never been
suspended. It was altogether a subservient Assembly, submissive
to the dictates of the usurping civil authority. Dr George Cook,
who had lost the leadership of the Assembly in 1833 now came
back to power and succeeded in winning approval for a
reactionary policy. Cook's right-hand man was James Robertson
of Ellon, a Moderate with certain evangelical leanings. Robertson
was fully awake to the abuses of Patronage, but he disfavoured
the Veto Act as a means of dealing with them. As it happened,
however, the formation of the Free Church of Scotland had the
effect of making Patronage more intolerable in the Church which
had supported it. For the outgoing of so many excellent ministers,
and the loss of such a large number of probationers to the Free
Church meant that in the famine conditions which arose many
men were admitted to the vacant pastorates of the Church of
Scotland who had little qualification for the holy office of the
ministry, and who had so little appeal to the people that the
power of the Patrons was often fully strained in order to secure

their induction to pastoral charges. A Bill, sponsored by Lord Aberdeen, and acquiesced in by the Church, gave the communicant members of a vacant parish the right to lodge objections of any kind whatsoever against a presentee, the Presbytery to be sole judge of the objections. This right of objection came to be so freely exercised by the people that by 1869 the Assembly resolved to petition Parliament to end Patronage. But it was not until 1874 that, under a Conservative government, a Bill was passed to end the right of patrons and grant the people the freedom to choose their own ministers.

But more of that later.

In the years following the Disruption feeling ran so high in ecclesiastical circles that unseemly rivalries ensued. The ministers who had remained in the Established Church found it hard to strike a heroic pose, yet many of them regarded themselves as more truly the martyrs of the hour than their disinherited brethren who, notwithstanding their losses in respect of the temporalities, were rich in popular esteem. Never was the term "Moderate" more charged with opprobrium than in those years, and its application to the Established clergy was made almost without distinction. Yet there were men of balanced judgment who recognised that the distinctions were there, and who saw the wrongness of not acknowledging them. One of Dr John Bruce's admirers, for instance, who had not heard his first sermon after the Disruption, was rather upset by a somewhat garbled report that she had heard of it.

"Dr Bruce," she said, when he visited her a few days later, "I hope ye didna say what they say ye said last Sabbath."

"And what was that?" asked Dr Bruce.

"They tellt me that ye said that not a good man and not a wise man stayed in the Established Kirk," was the reply.

Bruce shook his head protestingly and gave her the true version: "No, no woman, I didn't say that. On the contrary, I said that there were still good men and wise men in the Established Kirk, but that *the good men who stayed in were not wise, and the wise men who stayed in were not good!*"

It is an understatement that there were many in the Free Church, and in other non-established communions, who would have agreed with his estimate!

Some of the Evangelicals who stayed in the Established Church justified their decision on the plea that they were still as free to preach the Gospel as ever they had been. But the apostolic Dr John MacDonald, of Ferintosh, had his own comment in this connection. "Had I remained in the old Church," he said at the October 1843 Free Church General Assembly, "I might preach the doctrines I had been preaching for eight and thirty years, but

65

how could I go to the Lord for His presence to accompany my ministrations and render them effectual when He could cast in my face that I had denied the headship of Christ over the Church?"[1]

Going to Christ without the camp always involves the bearing of His reproach. The Evangelicals who formed the Free Church of Scotland had taken this into their reckoning when they counted the cost, and the relentless opposition with which they had to contend after the Disruption became an accomplished fact caused them no surprise — unless, perhaps, in the baseness of the methods used to suppress them. This opposition came in the main from the thwarted patrons, chagrined that their petty despotism had been successfully challenged. The refusal of sites for new buildings appeared to be the settled policy of the landed proprietors, with a few notable exceptions. Sir George Sinclair of Thurso relented to the extent of permitting the Free Church to build on his estates, *but only on waste land*! Others compromised by permitting erections of a temporary character, or by offering sites at such a distance from the people as to be quite unsuitable. At Kilmallie the only site permitted them was a piece of bog-land which the proprietor felt sure they would never use. But they did, and by unsparing exertion they made it suitable to their purpose and built their church there. Sir James Riddell of Strontian — himself an Episcopalian — refused the Free Church a site on any part of his estates. But again the proprietor underrated the determination and ingenuity of his Free Church tenants, for they built themselves a floating church in a Clyde shipbuilding yard and anchored it in Loch Sunart where it served as a church and a school until an exceptionally high tide lifted it from its anchorage and deposited it safely on the shore. Sir James afterwards relented, and a Free Church place of worship was built on a suitable site.

Reference was made at the Glasgow Assembly in 1843 to correspondence between the Duke of Sutherland and some of his tenants regarding the refusal of sites. Mr Makgill Crichton read a letter from the Duke's Commissioner, James Loch — the notorious Loch of the Sutherland evictions — in which he replies to representations made to his ducal master. The Duke, he avers, "believes that there is no difference in doctrine between those who have left the Establishment and those who have adhered to it, and that the separation has been carried out upon principles not founded on any distinction of religious belief, but for widely different reasons, which several of the secession have not hesitated to avow, and upon which some have not failed to act, namely, a determination to pull down and destroy the Establishment. . . ."

The sycophantic Commissioner is pained that any should

doubt the pure intentions of the Duke and assures the petitioners that they have been misled by a "bad adviser."

"The Duke's judgment and conscience," comments Mr Makgill Crichton, "declare to be trivial and unimportant the principles which the inhabitants of Sutherland, like their fathers before them, deem so sacred that, rather than relinquish them, they would suffer the spoiling of their goods and the shedding of their blood; therefore the Duke concludes that the people shall rule themselves by his Grace's conscience. I will only say that the King upon the throne would not dare to avow such principles as the rule over the consciences of his subjects, much less is the Duke of Sutherland entitled to maintain such a system of spiritual despotism over the people of that great province."[2]

For some of the congregations who were denied sites the Church provided large tents capable of containing from 200 to 700 persons. Five of these tents went to Sutherland.

The spirit of intolerance shown by the Duke of Sutherland was matched in the south by the Duke of Buccleuch. At Canonbie, for example, he refused a site to the Free Church congregation, numbering around 500 people, and when they erected a tent on a plot of waste moorland where camping facilities were allowed to tinkers and gipsies, they were ordered off, and throughout the winter of 1843-44 the congregation could find no place where to meet for worship except the high road which in those times would be almost entirely unfrequented on the Lord's Day.

Thomas Brown, a reporter from the front-line battle, has told in considerable detail, in his *Annals of the Disruption*, the story of the sufferings endured by the homeless pastors and their families, the churchless worshippers, and the teachers who were extruded from their office by the residuary Church of Scotland. But, as so often happens, persecution had the effect of strengthening the determination of the persecuted, and deepening sympathy for their cause. All over the country the necessary buildings were erected and the congregations were settled with the pastors of their choice. It was realised that the Free Church of Scotland had come to stay.

"Someone," says Dr Guthrie, who did magnificent work in the manse-building project, "a foe to our Church, said to a friend of mine in Glasgow, 'Well, we had some hope you would all go to pieces and be driven out to sea after the Disruption. When we saw you build churches, we had less hope; when we saw you build schools, we had less still; but when you have built your manses you will have dropped your anchor, and there will be no driving you out.' "[3]

The Free Church planned on the lines of the former Church of Scotland, whose testimony she was resolved to maintain and whose programme of service she was determined to follow out as far as her resources would allow. The aim of a church and school in every parish in Scotland was still the ideal which she kept before her, and with the high proportion of ministers, licentiates, students, lay-preachers and teachers who had adhered to her she was able to make a promising beginning. The Church of Scotland still had a majority of ministers and, on paper at least, the greater bulk of the people. But as against that, the ministers who had sacrificed their worldly all for the sake of the Gospel were obviously men with a burning zeal for its propagation in its purity, and the people who chose to be sharers of their reproach were clearly men and women whose loyalty would express itself in self-denying and consecrated service.

Within a year of the Disruption the Free Church had erected and equipped close on 500 churches — plain buildings, most of them, and put together with the haste that the situation demanded. But the Sanballats who had mocked at the beginning of their enterprise, saying "What do these feeble Jews?" and had circulated derisory cartoons in ridicule of the Free Church found that their puerile efforts had no arresting effect upon the industry and progress of her people.

If the gibe was true that

> The Free Kirk is the Wee Kirk,
> The Kirk without the steeple;

so too, in many parts of the country, was the counter-gibe that

> The Auld Kirk is the cauld kirk,
> The kirk without the people.

But such exchanges are but poor memorials of a great age.

Dr W. Garden Blaikie, the last of the Disruption Fathers to occupy the Moderatorial Chair of the Free Church General Assembly, recalling those stirring times, said, "The spirit of the Disruption was the spirit that gave all glory to Christ. It hovered much about Bethlehem and Nazareth, Gethsemane and Calvary, the cross and the crown, the empty tomb and the crown of glory. It warmed our Assemblies, it coloured our enterprises, it drew our hearts together, it sent us on our way rejoicing."[4]

1. *Proceedings of Free Church General Assembly;* Oct. 1843, p. 71.
2. ibid. pp. 93, 94.
3. D. A. Mackinnon, *Some Chapters in Scottish Church History;* pp. 212, 213.
4. ibid. p. 25.

CHAPTER ELEVEN

EBB-TIDE SETS IN

It was so much of the irony of history that a Church which had prided itself on the place that it gave to the Reformed Faith should so soon become the home of that revolutionary movement in Theology which has transformed the whole aspect of the religious life of Scotland.—*Principal John Macleod, D.D.*

Dr Garden Blaikie, in his Moderatorial address already quoted, assigns the early prosperity of the Free Church of Scotland to four principal causes: (1) "the earnest spiritual tone which marked it through and through"; (2) "the unity of heart and soul that bound all in one"; (3) "the intense activity shown in every department"; and (4) "the thorough organisation of the work." Yet long before that address was delivered the Free Church had begun to show disquieting signs of change. What had gone wrong? There was still "intense activity . . . in every department," and the organisation was as "thorough" as ever; but the earlier "earnest spiritual tone" and the "unity of heart and soul that bound all in one" were no longer in such clear evidence. The Free Church was changing, and many discerning and devout people in her membership feared that it was not for the better. What had produced the change?

The first and basic cause was, we may believe, *the pride of achievement*. The fears for the future of the Free Church, the haunting doubt that she would be able to survive, had been completely falsified. Beyond her own most sanguine expectations she had prospered. Her stand for spiritual independence and national righteousness had appealed to the people, and the numbers of her adherents continued to multiply. Evangelical churches throughout Christendom admired her and looked to her for spiritual leadership and example. She had succeeded in everything to which she had set her hand — in organisation, in administration, in education, in social activity, in missionary enterprise at home and abroad, and God had manifestly blessed her work. She was, in the best sense, a progressive Church, a Church that could get things done. But history repeated itself. "Jeshurun waxed fat and kicked."

It was as a shrewd discerner of the times that Dr Rainy told the General Assembly of 1887, with commendable concern, that "they had been guilty sometimes of making God's goodness to them as a Church the occasion of pride. At the Disruption," he said, "and in the days that followed, we had ground for the most copious and emphatic thanksgiving. We were as men that dreamed; and the Lord had done great things for us. Did we escape the temptation to turn this goodness into an occasion for arrogance and scorn? Looking back, I say no. We did not escape it. Therein we sinned."[2]

Another cause of decline, ironically enough, ensued from *the desire for ecclesiastical reunion*. The lamentable divisions of Scottish Presbyterianism were beginning to heal. The Secession Church of 1733 had split over the Burgess Oath in 1747 into Burghers and Anti-Burghers. These bodies divided again, the Burghers, in 1799, into Auld Licht Burghers and New Licht Burghers; and the Anti-Burghers in 1806 into Auld Licht Anti-Burghers and New Licht Anti-Burghers. Now the movement went into reverse. The Auld Licht Burghers returned to the Church of Scotland in 1839, to become part of the Free Church of Scotland in 1843. The New Licht Burghers and New Licht Anti-Burghers came together in 1820 to form the United Secession Church. In 1847 the Relief Church and the United Secession Church joined as the United Presbyterian Church. In 1852 the majority of the Auld Licht Anti-Burghers who had stood out from the union of 1806 joined the Free Church of Scotland.

Now it is not of the true spirit of Presbyterianism to rejoice in division, and when long-parted brethren decide to confer about the causes of disunion, with a view to removing them, the occasion is, and ought to be, one for praise and thanksgiving. But it is just at that point that care has to be exercised, for too often it has happened that in such negotiations the zeal for reunion has induced a spirit of compromise in which agreements are reached that blur vital principles and override the teaching of the Holy Scriptures — that teaching that must always be regulative of the Church's life and doctrine if she is to enjoy Divine blessing in her work.

It was this unguarded zeal for ecclesiastical reunion that wrought such havoc in the Free Church towards the end of the 19th century, at the very time when she was celebrating the jubilee of her formation.

Along with this move for ecclesiastical reunion, and closely related to it, was the ambition — by no means confined to the Free Church — to eclipse the Established Church. The ambition was understandable in the circumstances of the time. In many parishes the bulk of the people belonged to the non-established churches, especially to the Free Church. It seemed not only ironical but unjust, therefore, that the people adhering to these churches should be taxed in the interests of the ministry of the Established Church from which they had separated themselves. A crusade for the disestablishment of the Church of Scotland was launched, and it gathered momentum with the passing years. Alarmed by this development, as well as by the unrest which Patronage was now creating within her own borders, the Church of Scotland initiated a move for the abolition of Patronage. It was Patronage that had caused the Secession of 1733, the Relief Secession of 1761 and that lay behind the Disruption of 1843. It was reasoned that if Patronage were now abolished the disestablishment crusade would run out of steam, and the people — especially those who adhered to the Free Church of Scotland — would return to the "pure Establishment" which Thomas Chalmers had desiderated in 1843.

The leaders of the Free Church disestablishment movement countered this move by appointing a Church and State Committee, under the convenership of Dr Robert Rainy, to keep in touch with Parliament in the matter. Disestablishment became a strong element in the move for reunion which was afoot among the non-established Presbyterian denominations. Parliamentary and ecclesiastical politics now became closely inter-twined. Assessing the movement for union between the Free Church of Scotland and the United Presbyterian Church, as early as 1870, Professor George Smeaton had said, "Politics have much to do with it — I fear much more than religion. It has moved forward in an atmosphere of strong political partisanship, and seems destined to be a tool, and a willing tool, for the purposes of mere party politicians. I tremble at the thought; for never does a Church make the religion of Jesus a mere means to an ulterior end of a worldly kind but it brings down a terrible Nemesis and visitation."[3]

The truth of that forecast was soon made fully evident. But above and beyond all other causes of spiritual deterioration in the Free Church of Scotland was *her changing attitude to the Holy Scriptures, and to the Westminster Confession of Faith* which for more than two centuries had been her principal subordinate Standard, and to which her office-bearers were pledged. This becomes clear as we follow out the story of ecclesiastical reunion in Scotland.

Although official steps for the uniting of the Free Church of Scotland and the United Presbyterian Church were not taken until 1863 there had been informal talks between members of both Churches with that end in view. The fact that the Synod of the United Presbyterian Church met earlier in the year than did the General Assembly of the Free Church meant that the initiative, officially, was taken by the former body. A committee was appointed to meet with any similar body that might be set up by the Free Church General Assembly and the Synods of the English Presbyterian Church, the Reformed Presbyterian Church, and the Original Secession Church to consider the question of union.

The Free Church General Assembly took reciprocal action. In the motion for the setting up of its committee the duty was recognised of aiming at the accomplishment of union "by all suitable means," but consistently with *a due regard to the principles of this Church."*

From the outset of negotiations it became evident that the conferring Churches differed widely in their conception of the relationship of Church and State. The United Presbyterian Church had assumed the Voluntary position, holding that it is not competent for the civil magistrate to give legislative sanction to any creed in the way of setting up a civil establishment of religion. The Free Church, on the other hand—although by force of circumstances virtually a Voluntary church and no longer enjoying the benefits of Establishment—had come out from the Establishment still holding to the Establishment Principle. Nor was this the only point of difference between them, for as discussions proceeded the fact emerged that the doctrinal position of the United Presbyterian Church was no longer that of the Secession Fathers in 1733, nor of the Reformed Church in Scotland from its earliest days. James Morison, a Secession minister in Kilmarnock, had been ejected from the Church because of his departure from the Calvinistic doctrine to which he was pledged by his ordination vows—particularly on the matters of Election and the extent of the Atonement. At his trial two of his former Professors, John Brown and Robert Balmer, stood by him with such determination as to attract suspicion to themselves. An endeavour was made to bring them both to trial, but Balmer died while the investigation was in its preliminary stages, and his colleague, Dr Brown, was in the end exonerated. The result was that the way was opened, as Principal John Macleod put it, "for the teaching of a doctrine of Atonement which admitted of a double substitution, one that was effective and redemptive, and the other that was provisional or conditional, or, as the issue would prove, ineffective."

Notwithstanding these differences, the pro-union party in the Free Church carried a motion in the General Assembly of 1867 to the effect that the differences between the conferring Churches constituted no bar to union between them. The result was that such prominent conservatives as Dr James Begg, Dr William Nixon, Dr Julius Wood and Dr James Gibson resigned from the Union Committee on the ground that the motion which the Assembly had approved implied "an abandonment and subversion of an

Locked Out: October 1900 (see page 108)

The Queen addresses the Assembly: May 1969

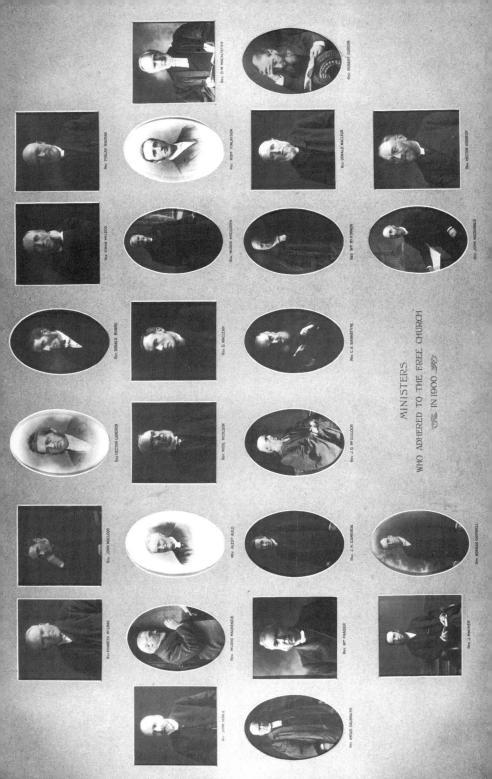

MINISTERS
WHO ADHERED TO THE FREE CHURCH
IN 1900

admittedly constitutional principle of the Free Church of Scotland."[4]

By 1871, opposition to the proposed union had become so widespread, that the Union Committee were instructed to restrict their attention to the question of closer co-operation between the Churches rather than union. But the Committee interpreted their remit more generously than was intended, and prepared a scheme of mutual eligibility, whereby ministers of the one Church could be called to charges in the other without any formal application of admission to the denomination. An influential minority, however, objected to this proposal as a subtle effort to effect union without binding declaration of identity of doctrine and principle.

Notwithstanding this objection, the proposal of the Union Committee commanded sufficient favour in the Presbyteries to produce a motion by Dr R. S. Candlish in the 1872 Assembly that the overture regarding mutual eligibility be passed into a standing law of the Church. But in the course of the year the Constitutionalists in the Church had not been idle. The recently formed Free Church Defence Association took steps to safeguard the Constitution of the Church, and *The Watchword,* under the vigorous editorship of Dr James Begg, powerfully supported by Dr Hugh Martin, brought the matters in dispute before the Church at large. The move for union seemed likely to end in the splitting of the Free Church. Legal opinion was sought as to the destination of the Church's property and endowments in the event of a disruption, and, in readiness for such an event, a building was hired prior to the meeting of the General Assembly to which the minority could withdraw to continue their witness and business.

Almost at the last moments, however, the minority accepted a modification of the proposal regarding mutual eligibility, to the effect that all ministers received into the Free Church under this provision should be required to avow their acceptance of the distinctive position of the denomination to which they sought admission. And with that the pro-unionists in the Free Church had to be content for the time being. Peace was restored, but most people knew it was a mere lull in the storm. It was around this time that Dr Robert Buchanan wrote to a friend, "I daresay *death* will have a good deal to do among us before the set time of union comes."[5]

He was right. Not until all the most outstanding Constitutionalist leaders who had championed the cause of the Free Church in those testing years were off the scene were the Union negotiations between the Free Church and the United Presbyterian Church resumed. From this time a new view began to emerge concerning the Church's relation to its professed creed. The Church, it was now argued, was entitled to claim the right of going

73

back on its pledged engagements and of taking a course that expediency and changing circumstances might suggest, irrespective of the assent by which each member of the Church was bound to its standards. It was an extreme and even revolutionary interpretation of the principle of Spiritual Independence.

The outstanding exponent of this new view was Dr Robert Rainy who had succeeded Dr William Cunningham as Professor of Church History in the New College, later becoming Principal in succession to Dr R. S. Candlish. The Union movement thus fostered in the Free Church a doctrinal fluidity that was at complete variance with the settled orthodoxy of earlier years. Principal Cunningham had sensed the beginnings of this change in his own time, and had deplored the Church's growing incompetence to estimate aright its true character. The tendency which Cunningham had detected was particularly dangerous, coming as it did at a time when, as Thomas Carlyle put it, men thought that they could "hold the premises of German unbelief and draw the conclusions of Scottish evangelical orthodoxy." The old evangelicalism of the Reformed Church was rapidly being infiltrated by the new liberalism. Cartesian Rationalism had, over a long period, been permeating the thinking of the Church, especially in the subjectivist form which had developed in Germany. A scepticism as to the supernaturalism of Holy Scripture began to show itself. No longer was it sufficient to regard a doctrine as true simply because the Bible affirmed it. Historical investigation must establish the facts presented in a manner that would satisfy man's reason. Inevitably, there came a whittling down of doctrine. Distinctions were made between the essentials and non-essentials of the Christian Faith, the difference being reached by a purely subjective process and, consequently, with confusing conclusions. Let the non-essentials go; the less there is to be defended as "essential" the stronger the defence will be! J. M. Shaw's *Essentials and Non-Essentials of the Christian Faith,* although belonging to a later phase of the controversy, and referring mainly to events in a different country, may be regarded as typical of the new school that had come into being. In the final analysis Shaw's "essentials" do not themselves appear to be particularly essential!

What was called the "modern mind" came to be regarded as the ultimate criterion in the judgment of doctrine; and yet a more variable standard of judgment could hardly be conceived. For, as B. B. Warfield writes in his review of Denney's *The Atonement and the Modern Mind,* "There is, after all, but one 'mind' to be considered, and this is the human mind; and the human mind is fundamentally much the same in modern times as it has always been, and is accessible to much the same rational and emotional appeal. . . . We are deeply thankful that Dr Denney expounds the Atonement to us so richly and so truly. But we look at his foundations and can see no reason why he should be so sure he is right; and we see no reason why tomorrow he may not expound to us something which may happen 'to find him'—with equal confidence and equal inconsequence."[6]

Dr J. I. Packer says truly that "subjectivist principles, if consistently worked out, would destroy supernatural Christianity. If the human mind is set up as the measure and test of truth, it will quickly substitute for man's incomprehensible Creator a comprehensible idol fashioned in man's own image; man wants a god he can manage and feel comfortable with, and will inevitably invent one if allowed. He will forget (because he cannot understand) the infinite gulf that separates the Creator from His creatures, and will picture to himself a god wholly involved in this world and wholly comprehensible (in principle at any rate) by the speculative intellect."[7]

By the last quarter of the nineteenth century the influence of the new Liberalism which had taken possession of the principal German schools began to reveal itself in the Free Church of Scotland, both in Church and classroom. Under pressure from current trends the Church had become less sure of herself and more receptive to the new learning. The Free Church must not be obscurantist! Her ministry must be second to none in intellectual attainment and breadth of scholarship! So, more and more, the custom grew of sending her most promising students to the seats of learning in Germany which had been taken over by the Higher Critical movement.

Now this zeal for scholarship was good up to a point. Obscurantism is not to be equated with orthodoxy, and the Church that fails to keep herself abreast of advances in scholarship is assuming an attitude that is unworthy of her high calling. But her thinking must always be governed by reverence, and she must never permit herself to forget that the "things most surely believed"—the doctrines committed to her keeping—were not devised by man's wisdom, but given by revelation from God. The Holy Scriptures are self-authenticating and will bear the test of investigation, but the grasp of Reason will always come short of the reach of Faith.

It was a pious platitude of the Higher Critical school from the beginning that the authority on which we must build is not the Bible but Christ; not a Book but a Person. Professor B. B. Warfield shows the falsity of this antithesis in his review of Denney's book on the Atonement already referred to. He wonders how Denney, on his view of Scripture, "expects to convince any man that the theory (of the Atonement) he sets forth is true. He does not know that there was a teacher sent from God named Jesus except on testimony that to us in the last resort is the bare testimony of Scripture; he does not know that this man died for our sins except simply on the word of this Jesus: he does not know that this death was acceptable to God and atones for sin, or how it atones for sin, or how it is made available for us—or anything that enters into the essence of the transaction—except on the bare authority of Scripture. He does not know one tenth-part of what he has told us about the Atonement, and what he insists upon as constituting its very heart, except on the faith of those very Scriptures to which he will accord no real authority. When at the close of the book he tells us, to clinch the matter, 'And I am very sure that in the New Testament' the exercise of trust in Christ 'is first and fundamental,' it appeals to *us*; but we resent it a little from *him*. *He* has given himself no right to urge that argument."[8]

The Higher Criticism made a quiet, even furtive, entrance into the academic life of the Free Church of Scotland through Professor A. B. Davidson who was appointed to the Old Testament chair in the New College, Edinburgh, in 1870, in succession to the saintly and scholarly Dr (Rabbi) John Duncan whose assistant he had been since 1863. Davidson was a man of wide culture and learning withal of such caution and personal charm that only a most sensitive ear would have detected a false note in his teaching. But when his brilliant pupil, William Robertson Smith, became, at the age of 24, Professor of Old Testament at the Aberdeen College of the Free Church the hidden heresy was brought out into the open and recklessly expounded. Robertson Smith had studied under Albrecht Ritschl and others of the Critical school in Germany, and later became acquainted with Julius Wellhausen whose revolutionary ideas about the authorship of the Pentateuch he made largely his own. Articles on the Bible which Smith later wrote for the *Encyclopaedia Britannica* were so manifestly in Higher Critical strain that proceedings were taken against him in the Courts of the Church. But so widely had the Higher Criticism spread in the Church by then that the process dragged on for years; and even when a decision was eventually reached it was by no means a clear-cut repudiation of the unorthodox views which had raised the issue. One speaker indeed pointed out that it "dealt with the heretic but not with the heresy." The motion was by Dr Rainy, and it said, "The General Assembly, having the responsible duty of overseeing the teaching in the Divinity Halls, while they are sensible of the importance of guarding the due liberty of professors, and encouraging learned and candid research, feel themselves constrained to declare that they no longer consider it safe or advantageous for the Church that Professor Smith should continue to teach in one of her colleges."[9]

Robertson Smith was removed from his chair but his heretical views were allowed to remain. Within a short time of his departure some 300 of his friends and supporters—among whom were several future leaders of the Church—met and passed the following resolution: "We declare that the decision of the Assembly leaves all Free Church ministers and office-bearers free to pursue the critical questions raised by Professor W. R. Smith, and we pledge ourselves to do our best to protect any man who pursues these studies legitimate."

One of these resolutioners, later Professor T. M. Lindsay, went further, and publicly committed himself to the main positions taken by Robertson Smith, at the same time challenging the Conservative party in the Church to take action against him. The fact that the challenge was not taken up is an indication of the extent to which the theological climate in the Free Church had changed. Charges of heresy were indeed brought at later times against Professor Marcus Dods, Professor A. B. Bruce, and Professor George Adam Smith, but little difficulty was experienced in delivering the men from their accusers. Principal Rainy, speaking in defence of Professors Bruce and Dods, declared that they must be allowed to "carry on their teaching in the class and elsewhere from their own convictions." The change of criterion was ominous. These teachers had solemnly professed, on being admitted to their chairs that they sincerely owned and believed "the whole doctrine contained in the Confession of Faith . . . to be founded upon the Word of God." and had promised "firmly and constantly" to "adhere thereto", and, to the utmost of their power, "assert, maintain, and defend the same." And yet, although their teaching had been shown to be subversive of the doctrine which they had vowed to adhere to "firmly and constantly," it was represented that their conscientious duty was to teach "from their own convictions," even though this should involve a departure from the vows which they had taken.

Gradually, "the way of the transgressor" was being made smooth. Men who faithfully contended for loyalty to ordination pledges were pilloried as disturbers of the peace, while those who claimed liberty to bend their vows in deference to the spirit of the new age were acclaimed as champions of the Church's freedom. To be a Constitutionalist was to be an obstructionist, and an intolerable nuisance. What could be done to curb them? Heresy trials were troublesome occurrences and had a very unsettling influence upon the life of the Church, for they kept alive the suspicion that there was a drift away from the Confessional position. The course of common honesty would have been to indicate clearly where they were at variance with the teaching of the *Confession,* but such a revelation would be risky, for it would show that what they were calling in question was not so much the doctrine of the *Confession* as that of the Holy Scriptures themselves. And there was still a sufficient concern for doctrinal soundness among the people to make that a hazardous procedure. There was a safer alternative. They would leave the *Confession* alone, but relax the terms by which ministers and other office-bearers in the Church were bound to it.

The visits of Dwight L. Moody and Ira D. Sankey to Scotland in 1873-74 made their own impact on the religious life of Scotland in this period of change. Moody was no precisian in theology. Professor (Rabbi) John Duncan's description of Brownlow North, the Scottish evangelist, as "an untrained theologue" with the emphasis on "theologue" could not be applied to him. "Theologue" he was not; "untrained" he certainly was. To describe his teaching as "Arminian"—as some writers do—is to put too fine a point on it. It was more of the patch-work quilt variety, and the patches bore little evidence of skilled selection. But Moody was a highly gifted man, and his grasp of the cardinal verity of salvation by faith in a crucified Saviour, together with his burning zeal in proclaiming it, made him a commanding voice among the multitudes. Dr W. M. MacGregor, in a sermon on the Union of 1900 preached to his congregation in Free St Andrew's Church, Edinburgh, says of him, "Within our generation there has been no force so powerful or so wholesome in the Free Church as Moody, who gave our preaching a new complexion, who carried hymns and instruments with a rush, and who openly condemned the long prayers and services to which we had been accustomed. He came upon us like a breath of God's air from outside."[10]

Scotland was having its first experience of American mass evangelism and was finding it exciting. The musical part of the meetings, the rousing hymns, the catchy choruses, and especially the solos of Ira D. Sankey proved an acceptable novelty and added greatly to the appeal of the gatherings. But it was, as Principal Macleod reminds us, "the day of ebb-tide, and the definite out-and-out Calvinism of another day was going out of fashion and yielding place to a presentation of the Gospel which, without being pronouncedly Arminian, avoided the emphasis which the older Evangelicals laid on the New Birth as a Divine intervention. This modified message put its emphasis on the need the sinner has of forgiveness to the eclipse of the equally urgent need that he has of regeneration."

The Evangelicals in the ministry were divided over the movement. Some welcomed it because, whatever its irregularites, it gave prominence to the theme of "Christ and Him crucified," and hoped that it would prove the correction of the false gospel which had come into vogue through the Liberal theology. Others—and Dr

John Kennedy, of Dingwall, was prominent among them—detected a false note in the new evangelism in the respect that it failed to make clear the total inability of fallen man and the all-sufficiency of Divine grace, and they were openly critical of it.

On the other hand, many of the advocates of change, like Dr MacGregor himself, gave the new evangelism an enthusiastic welcome. This was the very climate in which the new theology could advance. Creeds were at a discount. Doctrinal distinctions were of little significance. Denominational differences and distinctive principles scarcely mattered. The new movement worked. It was fruitful in "results". The inquiry-rooms totted up large numbers of converts. Its very success branded the older Reformed evangelism as effete. A wind of change was sweeping through the Church which would carry away the dust and cobwebs of the centuries. The old order must yield to the new.

But the fears of some of the more discerning critics of the movement were not unfounded. Indeed, it seemed to them that the prophetic words of Thomas McCrie, spoken more than half a century before, were being fulfilled before their eyes. "A vague and indefinite evangelism," wrote Dr McCrie, "mixed with seriousness into which it is the prevailing disposition of the present age to resolve all Christianity, will, in the natural progress of human sentiment, degenerate into an insubstantial and incoherent pietism, which, after effervescing in enthusiasm, will finally settle into indifference, in which case the spirit of infidelity and irreligion, which is at present working and spreading to a more alarming extent than many seem to imagine, will achieve an easy conquest over a feeble and exhausted and nerveless adversary."

Such was the mood of the hour when Scottish Presbyterianism set itself to the task of ecclesiastical reunion.

From the tone of the speeches given by some of the distinguished visitors who addressed the Jubilee Assembly of the Free Church in 1893 it was evident that this drift from Reformed doctrine was causing concern to those who had rejoiced in the unambiguous testimony of the Free Church in earlier years. Dr Alexander Maclaren of Manchester fastened on one of the current slogans in the course of his address. "We have heard very much of late," he said, "about the return of this generation to Jesus Christ as the centre of all our religion. But, but what Christ is it that we are going back to? Is the historical Christ the incarnate Christ? Is your historical Christ the divine Christ? Is your historical Christ the Christ who died on the cross for the sins of the world? Is your historical Christ the risen, ascended, royal Christ? Then, then I say, back to *that* Christ; *there* is life. He that goeth beyond, and continueth not in the teaching of Christ, however he may fancy himself progressive, is retrograding. . . . A Church that has a

Christ but not a cross is perilously apt to have a name to live and be dead."[11]

The Moderator of the Presbyterian Church in Ireland made his references to current events in the Free Church so pointed as to evoke cries of disapproval from some of the commissioners. There had sometimes been rather a rough handling of the Scriptures, he said, "an emphasising of the human element rather than the divine; the magnifying of discrepancies into contradictions—in a word, there had been in connection with this criticism (the Higher Criticism) what he would call, not assurance, but cock-assurance."

But it was when he came to the cases of libel that had been before the Free Church and criticised the settlements which had been reached that the displeasure of some in his audience became noisiest of all. "In these settlements," he said, "there was more regard to the reaching of a majority than to the issuing of judgments upon the truth concerned."[12]

Tactless speaking, perhaps, but as events proved, only too tragically true.

1. D. A. Mackinnon, *Some Chapters in Scottish Church History;* pp. 203, 204.
2. James Moffatt, *The Presbyterian Churches;* p. 208.
3. Stewart and Cameron, *Free Church of Scotland 1843-1910;* pp. 18, 19.
4. ibid. p. 25.
5. ibid. p. 49.
6. B. B. Warfield, *Critical Reviews;* p. 103.
7. J. Packer, *Fundamentalism and the Word of God;* p. 171.
8. B. B. Warfield, *Critical Reviews;* p. 103.
9. *Proceedings of Free Church General Assembly,* 1881.
10. W. M. MacGregor, *What a Church lives for;* p. 11.
11. *Proceedings of Free Church Assembly,* 1893; p. 97.
12. ibid. p. 113.

CHAPTER TWELVE

CREEDS AND CONFESSIONS

Our ordination vow taking us bound to our Confession settles that we have a Constitution, clearly enough defines it, renders us answerable to it, and pledges the Church reciprocally as amenable to it also.—*Dr Hugh Martin.*

The question of creed subscription occupies so large a place in the study of the events discussed in these pages that it merits a chapter to itself. What is the influence of confessional statements in the life of the Church? Is it for good or evil? Is a credal statement really a bond of union, or is it more accurate to regard it as a cause of division?

These questions call for consideration.

From the opening words of the Gospel by Luke it may be inferred that the formulation of the Church's belief was early recognised as a necessary activity. The work of setting forth in order a declaration of the "things most surely believed" had evidently been attempted by many even before Luke took pen in hand to write to Theophilus, that he might know the certainty of those things wherein he had been instructed. The Church of Jesus Christ has been, and, in the nature of things, must always be, a confessional body. As the Divinely appointed "pillar and ground of the truth" she is under obligation to her Founder to present the manifesto of His Kingdom from age to age. And because the faith that she professes came by revelation of the Holy Spirit it is to be dogmatically proclaimed. But dogmatic proclamation calls for careful formulation, and in the great credal statements of the Christian Church we have the productions of devout and acute minds which, over the ages, were engaged in the work of giving precise expression to the fundamentals of Christian belief.

"Creeds and Confessions there must be," writes Principal W. A. Curtis. "Faith, having soul of religion, though it embraces more than intellect . . . cannot renounce the intellect . . . or dispense with words and forms of thought. . . . There cannot be a Gospel, or preacher's tidings for the saving of mankind, without an antecedent creed or body of belief, articulate or inarticulate. . . . It is in truth unthinkable that the vast aggregate of doctrinal symbols evolved by the Christian Church in all lands during nineteen centuries of intense activity should have proceeded from any but a profoundly natural and honourable instinct in the soul of faith."

It is to be feared, however, that much of what interest there is in creeds and confessions in times of spiritual disloyalty has little connection with any desire for a clearer understanding of the Church's faith, or for a more Biblical formulation of her doctrine. The phrase *ecclesia reformata semper reformanda est,* which formerly expressed the Church's concern that her doctrine should be, at all times, truly Reformed, and that the unfinished work of the Reformation should continue to be faithfully prosecuted, has been taken over by leaders of ecumenical movements who use it to urge the virtual pulping of all the historic formularies of the Faith as a necessary part of the process of producing a minimal symbol on which all branches of the Christian Church, and, eventually, perhaps some of other faiths, may be brought into agreement. The affliction of Erasmus, who had "little stomach for assertions," has always been prevalent in some measure or other, in the theological world. Many, indeed, have favoured the idea of dispensing with all credal statements. The Dutch Remonstrants in the early seventeenth century opposed Confessions on the allegation that they violated the authority of Holy Scripture and interfered with the freedom of conscience; furthermore, that they hindered advancement in knowledge and understanding. The English Unitarians of last century took rather similar ground, Dr James Martineau, for instance, alleging that credal formulations prejudged the convictions of posterity. The Non-Subscribing Party in the Irish Presbyterian Church had already taken the same position—not, they protested, because they disbelieved the doctrines contained in the *Westminster Confession of Faith,* but because creeds and confessions were "human tests of Divine truth."

Such views of creed formulation and subscription reveal an entire misconception of the purpose of confessional statements. Far from hindering growth in the knowledge of Biblical doctrine, they have provided helpful guidelines for advancement in an understanding of the essentials of the Faith. It is not claimed for them that they partake of the inerrancy of the Holy Scriptures whose teaching they systematise and exhibit; on the contrary, they are regarded as being properly subject to examination, and to revision, if it be found at any time that they fail adequately to express the true meaning of Scripture at any point covered. It was their overwhelming desire to be thoroughly Biblical in their formulations that led the compilers of the *Scots Confession* to write, in the introduction to their work, "We conjure you, if any man will note in this our Confession, any article or sentence repugnant to God's Holy Word, that it would please him of his gentleness, and for Christian charity's sake, to admonish us of the same in writing; and we, upon our honour and fidelity, do promise him satisfaction from the Holy Scriptures, or due reformation of that which he shall prove to be amiss."[2]

A similar spirit is expressed in the vow under which the Westminster Divines formulated their *Confession:* "I do seriously promise and vow, in the presence of Almighty God, that in this Assembly, whereof I am a member, I will maintain nothing in point of doctrine but what I believe to be most agreeable to the Word of God."[3]

Confessions drawn up with such painstaking care ought not to be lightly set aside.

The history of Confessions in the New Testament Church is a long one. It is impossible to be precise as to the time of their origin, but it is clear that from early times converts to the faith were required to express their agreement with the cardinal tenets of that faith before they received the initiatory rite of Christianity. Hence Philip's reply to the query of the Ethiopian eunuch, "What doth hinder me to be baptised?" "If thou believest with all thine heart thou mayest." Then followed the confession, "I believe that Jesus Christ is the Son of God". It may well be that it was already customary for converts to Christianity to profess their faith in some such formula as this. The words are simple, but their theological implications are profound.

A more expanded form of credal statement became necessary as the Church progressed with her missionary programme and won numerous converts from other faiths. Some of these brought elements of their former faiths into the Christian community, and it became imperative, especially after the passing of the Apostles and the senior members of the fellowship, to formulate the Church's faith in terms that would clearly and concisely set forth what she expected her members to believe and profess. Only thus could she bring out the distinction between what was orthodox and what was heterodox, and preserve the purity of life and doctrine that was so vital to the Church. To say, as some Liberal theologians of more recent times have said, that it is not doctrine that counts but life, is—to quote a speaker at the Edinburgh Calvinistic Congress of 1938—"about as sensible a slogan for the Church as it would be for the National Fitness Campaign to have, 'It is not nourishment that counts, but health'."[4]

It was the pressure of heretical doctrines that produced, in the course of the centuries, the more elaborate formularies of the historic Church Councils. Questions as to the true deity and humanity of Christ, the unity of His personality and the relationship of His two natures; the personality of the Holy Spirit and His place in the Godhead; these and many cognate problems sent men back to the Holy Scriptures to examine in their light the matters raised. The result of their toils we have in the creeds of the great ecumenical councils. These, however, were ante-dated by the so called *Apostles' Creed*—certainly in its older form as the *Roman Creed*—which, if not Apostolic in respect of antiquity, is nevertheless a remarkable epitome of Apostolic teaching. As a breviate of early Christian doctrine it is of the utmost significance. The pseudo-Christianity of rival systems compelled the Church, almost from the dawn of her history, to set forth the tenets of her faith in confessional form for the instruction of her members, the enlightenment of those whose faith had been unsettled by the doubts cast upon beliefs commonly held and for the reclamation of those who had committed themselves to unorthodox positions.

Objections to credal formularies are to be considered in the light of the fact that although the Church is an organism it necessarily reveals itself in an organisational pattern. And like every other organisation of human society, it must, for the orderly prosecution of its work and the prevention of confusion, have recognised articles of association.

The use of Confessional statements also serves to perpetuate sound doctrine, for thereby one generation transmits to another the body of teaching which it professes, and the principle of continuity which is proper to the Church's doctrinal statements is thereby honoured. And this, in no way, prejudges the convictions of posterity, for it is surely the duty of each generation in the Church to bring their religious thinking to the test of Holy Scripture. Nothing but good could possibly accrue to the Church if her ministers and other office-bearers were to examine afresh the doctrines to which they have pledged themselves, and reassure themselves, like the Bereans of long ago, as they bring their beliefs to the touch-stone of the Word, that "these things are so."

The objection to the use of Confessional standards on the allegation that it fosters the spirit of division in the Church cannot be seriously entertained. For division usually arises when office bearers, pledged to the Church's *Confession,* resile from their pledge and still expect to be left in full possession of the privileges which their engagement secured for them. But Ralph Erskine was undoubtedly right when he wrote, "Let them bear most the charge of schism that divide most from the Head, Jesus Christ, and from the Truth as it is in Him. . . . When defection becomes general, then division becomes a necessary duty and a great mercy; otherwise all would run into the gulf of defection together, making peace and pretensions to brotherly love a grave for burying all zeal for God and His truths and interest."

The preservation of Biblical doctrine in the Church is infinitely more important than the creation of an inclusivist body which lacks the basic marks of a true Church.

Objections to the use of creeds and confessions come also from those in the Church who regard it as a mark of superior intelligence to dispense with dogmatic statements of the faith, and who represent opponents of the Church's creeds as the emancipators of the age who have been raised up to deliver the Church from the offence of "symbololatry", as they call it. Doubt is more highly lauded than faith, and Tennyson's couplet is often quoted as if it were the last word in the matter;

> *There is more faith in honest doubt,*
> *Believe me, than in half the creeds.*

Faith and doubt may indeed be in conflict in the one heart, and the number of Christians whose hearts have not, at one time or another, been the arena of such conflicts must be relatively small. But if the doubter is to be classed as "honest" he will not bind himself by solemn ordination vows, nor continue to be bound, if his convictions have changed, to a profession of doctrines of which he stands in doubt.

Every Church has the right to require of its office-bearers that they sincerely signify their acceptance of the particular credal standards that represent the belief and testimony of that body, and the obligations of Creed subscription are much too weighty and sacred to be assumed with mental reservations.

The signatories of the *Auburn Affirmation,* in the Presbyterian Church in the United States of America came under severe castigation from an unexpected quarter when a group of Unitarians, headed by the former President Charles Eliot of Harvard, wrote, "With all courtesy and consideration, let us make it plain that religious teachers who play with words in the most solemn relations of life, who make their creeds mean what they were not originally intended to mean, or mentally reject a formula of belief while outwardly repeating it, cannot expect to retain the allegiance of men who are accustomed to straight thinking and square dealing."

It was inevitable that the Reformation of the 16th century should be productive, in the various countries affected by it, of several freshly-minted credal formularies setting forth anew the fundamental truths of New Testament Christianity which had been obscured, and even deliberately perverted, by a Church which had taken the mind and conscience of the people into its own authoritarian custody, claiming to be the only interpreter of Holy Scripture and the sole dispenser of spiritual grace. The impressive harmony of these Reformed symbols proves that those who were responsible for their production drew from a common source and worked to a common aim. There is no need to dispute with John Row when he claims for the Scottish Reformers that "they took not their pattern from any kirk in the world; no, not from Geneva itself," for the similarity between the *Confession* which they drew up, and the other Reformed symbols is explained when Row further says that "laying God's Word before them (they) made reformation according thereunto, both in doctrine first and then in discipline."

It is significant that when the agitation for credal relaxation arose in Scotland, as well as in other countries, it originated in a movement away from the binding authority of Holy Scripture itself. Professor J. Gresham Machen, writing on similar developments in American Presbyterianism, declares, "a man who solemnly accepts that system of doctrine (viz. the *Westminster Confession*) cannot at the same time be an advocate of a non-doctrinal religion which regards as a trifling thing that which is the very sum and substance of the *Confession* and the very centre and core of the Bible upon which it is based."

"The matter"—to continue with Machen—"may be made plain by an illustration from secular life. Suppose in a political campaign in America there be formed a Democratic Club for the purpose of furthering the cause of the Democratic Party. Suppose there are certain other citizens who are opposed to the tenets of the Democratic Club, and in opposition desire to support the Republican Party. What is the honest way for them to accomplish this purpose? Plainly, it is simply the formation of a Republican Club which shall carry on propaganda in favour of Republican principles. But suppose instead of pursuing this simple course of action, the advocates of Republican principles should conceive the notion of making a declaration of conformity to Democratic principles, thus gaining an entrance into the Democratic Club, and finally turning its resources into an anti-Democratic propaganda. That plan might be ingenious. But would it be honest? Yet it is exactly such a plan which is adopted by advocates of a non-doctrinal religion who by subscription to a creed gained an entrance into the ministry of doctrinal or evangelical Churches."[5]

But what then? Does this mean that a Church must be held as bound for all time to a Confession that it no longer accepts? It certainly does not; but it does mean that, in seeking amendment, honest methods should be followed. For if the Confessional position becomes a bondage to any man who is subject to it, he is in that position by his own voluntary action. He had every opportunity to study beforehand the vows that office-bearers are expected to take and the formula that they are required to sign. He is under no obligation to pledge himself to an acceptance of that position, and therefore, if he has given his pledge, he has no reason afterwards to complain of his ordination engagements as constituting a bondage.

But suppose that the ordinand pledged his vows in good faith, but afterwards fell out of agreement with the doctrinal position to which he had assented; what then? Is his only choice that between continuing in office with mental reservations regarding the doctrines of which he now stands in doubt, and simple resignation of office? Not at all. He is at full liberty, and indeed under moral obligation, to seek relief from the unhappy position in which he finds himself.

Discussing such a situation as this, Principal John Macleod cites the case of the celebrated American divine, Dr Archibald Alexander of Princeton, who, in his early ministry, became involved in some difficulties concerning baptism. The course that he followed was to acquaint his Presbytery with his problem, and to request from them a temporary exemption from acting against his present judgment. His request was granted, and, following a more intensive study of the matters which troubled him, his difficulties were all removed.

The case of Dr Alexander Anderson of Boyndie and Old Aberdeen, also referred to by Principal Macleod was different. Dr Anderson had also developed views regarding baptism which differed from Confessional teaching. But in taking the matter to his Presbytery he moved that the standards be so altered as to meet the views to which he had come. His arguments failed to convince his brethren, whereupon he resigned his charge and joined the Baptist communion.

These two cases had different results, but both Archibald Alexander and Alexander Anderson faced their difficulties in an honest and honourable way. The standards of the Church were treated with the respect due to them, and the ethics of creed subscription were fully maintained. If an ordinand, on the other hand, chooses to follow the alternative course, resiling from the system of doctrine to which he first pledged himself, and yet continuing in the service of the Church which admitted him to office, he brings dishonour upon himself—a dishonour in which his brethren also become involved if, knowing of his change of mind, they permit him to continue in an office to which he is no longer entitled.

Our Scottish Reformers were right when they made Discipline one of the marks by which the true Church is to be discerned. It is true, as the *Westminster Confession* puts it, that "the purest Churches under heaven are subject both to mixture and error" and no Church shall reach perfect purity in this world. But that fact is no argument for not striving towards the mark. It is thus that she grows in grace and influence. For a Church is spiritually powerful in proportion as she is doctrinally pure.

1. W. A. Curtis, *History of Creeds and Confessions;* pp. 431, 432.
2. *Scots Confession,* Preface.
3. *Westminster Confession of Faith.* Vow imposed upon Members of Assembly.
4. *Proceedings of Calvinistic Congress 1938;* p. 107.
5. J. G. Machen, *Christianity and Liberalism;* p. 169.

CHAPTER THIRTEEN

THE DECLARATORY ACT CONTROVERSY

**The Confession of Faith, with, and without, the
Declaratory Acts, are two not only different, but
essentially different, theologies.**—*Dr J. Stewart,
Templeton.*

Reference to such a measure as a Declaratory Act requires a preliminary word of definition. The main purpose of such an Act is, as indeed its name suggests, to declare, where ambiguity or dubiety exists, or is alleged to exist, what the General Assembly understands to be the true meaning of the passage, or passages, cited from its Standards as being of uncertain import. Thus, when by Act XII 1846, the Free Church General Assembly amended the *Questions and Formula to be used at the licensing of Probationers, and the Ordination of Deacons, Elders and Ministers respectively*, the Assembly took occasion "to declare, that, while the Church firmly maintains the same Scriptural principles as to the duties of nations and their rulers in reference to true religion and the Church of Christ, for which she has hitherto contended, she disclaims intolerant or persecuting principles, and does not regard her Confession of Faith, or any portion thereof, when fairly interpreted, as favouring intolerance or persecution, or consider that her office-bearers, by subscribing it, profess any principles inconsistent with liberty of conscience and the right of private judgment."[1]

There we have an instance of Declaratory legislation properly used. Its purpose is to clear up any uncertainty that may have arisen in connection with the matter dealt with. Properly used, it cannot bring in new legislation, nor can it amend existing legislation. To put it quite simply, a Declaratory Act is merely an explanatory Act. To use it as a means of introducing doctrinal changes, as was done in the movement for union between the Free Church of Scotland and the United Presbyterian Church, is to go beyond the powers originally conferred by the General Assembly. But that was exactly what the uniting bodies did.

The United Presbyterian Church led the way. Prior to the union of 1847, when the United Secession Church and the Relief Church came together to become the United Presbyterian Church, the Secession branch had already been agitated by heresy trials, and, although steps had been taken to rehabilitate the Church in the confidence of her more conservative people, it was evident that the expulsion of James Morison of Kilmarnock had done little to deter his sympathisers who remained in the Church. The drift away from the Calvinism of earlier days continued, and in 1877, in response to a movement for creed revision, a Committee was formed to go into the whole matter. The result was the Declaratory Act of 1879, which Dr J. R. Fleming commends as "the first formulation of the points on which liberal Scottish Presbyterianism was prepared to modify the traditional Calvinism."[2]

Condemnation of the Church's dishonesty came from an unexpected quarter. One of her own ministers, David Macrae of Gourock, denounced the framers of the Declaratory Act as men who had resorted to "Jesuitical devices" in their work. Macrae's quarrel with them, however, was not that they were changing the old order but that they were doing so under the pretence of maintaining it! His attack was so violent and his theological views so extreme that the Church felt compelled to take action against him. He was suspended from office, and soon afterwards founded an independent church in Dundee. But Dr Fleming comments that this episode, "though regrettable, did not arrest real theological progress."[3]

Similar steps were now taken by the Free Church General Assembly. A Declaratory Act, very similar to the United Presbyterian Act of 1879, was approved by the Assembly in 1891 and sent down to the Presbyteries of the Church as an overture under the Barrier Act. This Act, dating back to 1697, was devised "for preventing any innovation, and for securing due deliberation and harmony in the enactment of new laws, and in the alteration of old ones."

Declaratory Acts may be passed without transmission to Presbyteries in terms of the Barrier Act, when it is generally agreed that the declaration is in accordance with the old law. But if there be much difference of opinion on the subject, and if the point enforced be new, in any considerable measure, to the existing Ministers and Ruling Elders, it has been held that before the passing of such an Act, an Overture on the subject ought to be transmitted to Presbyteries, in terms of the Barrier Act (*Free Church Practice*).

That there was "much difference of opinion on the subject" dealt with in the 1892 Act soon became very evident. The members of the Committee who had drafted the Act had bestowed great care on the wording chosen, and on a superficial reading it appeared to give no cause for alarm.

In view of the misuse that was subsequently made of

declarative statements it is worth reproducing the terms of the Declaratory Act referred to. It runs as follows:

"Whereas it is expedient to remove difficulties and scruples which have been felt by some in reference to the declaration of belief required from persons who receive licence or shall be admitted to office in this Church, the General Assembly, with consent of Presbyteries, declare as follows:

I. That in holding and teaching, according to the *Confession,* the Divine purpose of grace towards those who are saved, and the execution of that purpose in time,

"(a) This Church most earnestly proclaims, as standing in the forefront of the revelation of Grace, the Love of God, Father, Son and Holy Spirit, to sinners of mankind, manifested especially in the Father's gift of the Son to be the Saviour of the world, in the coming of the Son to offer himself a propitiation for sin, and in the striving of the Holy Spirit with men to bring them to repentance.

"(b) That this Church also holds that all who hear the Gospel are warranted and required to believe to the saving of their souls; and that in the case of such as do not believe, but perish in their sins, the issue is due to their own rejection of the Gospel call. That this Church does not teach, and does not regard the *Confession* as teaching, the fore-ordination of men to death irrespective of their own sin.

"(c) That it is the duty of those who believe, and one end of their calling by God, to make known the Gospel to all men everywhere for the obedience of faith. And that while the Gospel is the ordinary means of salvation for those to whom it is made known, yet it does not follow, nor is the *Confession* to be held as teaching, that any who die in infancy are lost, or that God may not extend His mercy, for Christ's sake, and by His Holy Spirit, to those who are beyond the reach of these means, as it may seem good to Him, according to the riches of His grace.

"II. That in holding and teaching, according to the *Confession of Faith,* the corruption of man's whole nature as fallen, this Church also maintains that there remains tokens of his greatness as created in the image of God; that he possesses a knowledge of God and of duty: that he is responsible for compliance with the moral law and with the Gospel; and that, although unable without the aid of the Holy Spirit to return to God, he is yet capable of affections and actions which in themselves are virtuous and praiseworthy.

"III. That this Church disclaims intolerant or persecuting principles, and does not consider her office-bearers, in subscribing the *Confession,* committed to any principles

91

inconsistent with liberty of conscience and the right of private judgment.

"IV. That while diversity of opinion is recognised in this Church on such points in the *Confession* as do not enter into the substance of the Reformed Faith therein set forth, the Church retains full authority to determine, in any case which may arise, what points fall within this description, and thus to guard against any abuse of this liberty to the detriment of sound doctrine, or to the injury of her unity and peace."[4]

On a cursory reading the Act appeared to be quite innocuous, but discerning critics were not deceived by the clever camouflage of its framers. They were well aware that the declaration in Section 1 (a) regarding the love of God to sinners was designed to give coverage to the party in the Church who were moving away from the doctrine of particular redemption to a modified Calvinism, if not to out and out Arminianism.

Again, the statement in Section I (b) that men are not fore-ordained to death "irrespective of their own sin" was not necessary, for the *Confession* itself states that those who are ordained to eternal death are so ordained "for their sin, to the praise of God's eternal justice." It is true that there was in vogue at the time a caricature of Calvinism such as Robert Burns expresses in *Holy Willie's Prayer*, where he speaks of God as sending,

> . . . *Ane to heaven and ten to hell:*
> *A' for thy glory,*
> *And no for ony guid or ill*
> *They've done afore Thee!*

But for the rebuttal of such a view it surely would have been better to turn to the more Biblical phraseology of the *Confession* where the teaching of Holy Scripture comes to light so much more clearly than it does in the vague and misleading terms of this declarative statement which, in fact, is a veiled attack on the doctrine of election and on Covenant theology.

Section 2 of the Act introduced a modification of the doctrine of the corruption of man's whole nature by the Fall. Man, it allows, is unable "without the aid of the Holy Spirit to return to God," yet, even in his fallen condition, he is "capable of affections and actions which in themselves are virtuous and praiseworthy."

Now, if all that a sinner needs for his salvation is "the aid of the Holy Spirit to return to God," the implication is that man, despite the Fall, has retained some measure of spiritual life, and is not "dead in trespasses and sins" as the Scriptures represent him to be. But the work of the Holy Spirit in the believer is very much more than a mere reformation; it is a complete

92

regeneration. "Ye must be born again." No one will deny that even unregenerate men are capable of virtuous and laudable actions; but these actions have the quality of goodness only in a relative sense, and do not in any way contribute to man's salvation. In this declarative clause we have again a modification of Confessional teaching in deference to the new theology which was moving away from the doctrines of sovereign and efficacious grace.

The purpose of Section 3 of the Declaratory Act was clearly to make the whole matter of the Civil Magistrate an "open question," and thus to remove an obstacle in the way of union between the Free Church and the United Presbyterians. The disclaimer of intolerant or persecuting principles was quite unnecessary, for this had already been done by the Free Church General Assembly in 1846.

The most objectionable section of the Declaratory Act of 1891 was kept to the last. Allowance is made for "diversity of opinion" on such points in the Confession as do not enter into "the substance of the Reformed Faith"; but no guidance is given as to which doctrines fall into this category, or into the alternative category. The Church arrogates to herself the right to determine from time to time "what points fall within this description," and leaves herself without fundamentals, without essentials and without discipline. What was regarded in a past generation as entering into the substance of the Reformed Faith may in the next generation be classified differently. Kenneth Moody Stuart in a criticism of the Declaratory Act rightly observes that "the result of this proposed process of modifying the Calvinistic and Pauline doctrines of the Westminster Confession is not uncertain. It has been done more than once (for these modifications of the Declaratory Act are no more new than are the doctrines of the Confession) and always with the same result, that the Churches which followed this course lost all their evangelical life and fervour. This result befell the former English Presbyterians, who became Socinians; the Irish Presbyterians, who became Arians; and the New England Puritan Churches, which became wholly Rationalistic."[5]

Opponents of the Declaratory Act were not deceived by its calculated ambiguity and vagueness. They urged that the course of common honesty for the critics of the *Confession* would be to show where they judged the *Confession* to be at variance with the Holy Scriptures in its teaching, and to specify clearly which Confessional statements they wished to change. But the challenge was not accepted, and for obvious reasons. Investigation would soon bring to light that what they were calling in question was not so much the teaching of the *Westminster Confession* as that of the Holy Scriptures themselves. And there was still sufficient concern for doctrinal soundness in the Church to make such an investigation a most hazardous procedure. The more devious method of the Declaratory Act was therefore chosen as a policy of prudence!

During the year that the draft of the Declaratory Act was under consideration by the Presbyteries of the Church, in accordance with the requirements of the Barrier Act, an organised opposition to it began to take shape. Overtures were sent to the General Assembly of 1893 from several Presbyteries and Synods craving that the Act be rescinded. On the motion of Principal Rainy, who probably under-estimated the seriousness, if not the strength, of the opposition, this crave was refused, and the Declaratory Act received the approval of the General Assembly by a large majority. Many dissents were tabled, and two ministers, Rev. Donald Macfarlane of Raasay, and Rev. Donald MacDonald of Shieldaig, seceded from the Church to form the Free Presbyterian Church of Scotland. Several students of the Church joined them, as did also a considerable number of people, particularly in the Highland area.

But opposition to the Declaratory Act was by no means ended by the Free Presbyterian secession. Overtures were before the Free Church Assembly in the following year craving its repeal. The crave was again refused, but the overtures were not without effect. The secession had been larger than Dr Rainy had expected, and it had not left him with the unchallenged mastery in the Free Church General Assembly for which he had hoped. A resolute, though not large, Constitutionalist party continued in the Church, and these would have to be dealt with before it would become safe to carry Church union negotiations to the next stage. Accordingly, he carried a placatory resolution through the Assembly of 1894, declaring that the 1892 Declaratory Act was merely a relieving measure, and that its provisions were not binding upon any who did not wish to avail themselves of the doctrinal relaxation which it allowed. Some who had previously opposed the Declaratory Act now expressed themselves as satisfied; but the more resolute Constitutionalists continued in unyielding opposition, protesting that the Act was incompetent legislation, disallowed by the very Constitution of the Church; and in any case that it was, and would continue to be, inoperative so long as the Questions and Formula which bound the office-bearers of the Church to the *Westminster Confession* remained unchanged. They would not yield to the blandishments of the supreme tactician, Dr Rainy, nor would they be driven out to join their brethren who had gone into secession. In a pamphlet written during the earlier Union controversy, Dr John Kennedy of Dingwall, addressing the pro-

94

union party in the Free Church, wrote, "Of one thing be assured, that, of your ministers, elders, deacons and people, not a few are resolved not to forsake the banner of the Free Church, and are resolved too, not to separate from you till you have parted from them by being actually incorporated with those whose fellowship you have preferred. They will adhere to you as long as they can, and if there is to be a disruption, the act shall be yours, and all Christendom shall know that it is."[6]

Dr Kennedy and his stalwart fellow-Constitutionalists of the former union controversy were gathered to their fathers before the pro-union party in the Free Church made their next move. And when they did it was to find that there were still men in the Free Church, few in number though they now were, who were resolved, whatever the cost, to continue the Constitution and witness of the Free Church of Scotland. These men were not opposed to creed revision, where that could be shown, by reference to the Holy Scriptures to be called for, but they saw the dangers of the course on which the "progressives" in the Church were now embarking. "It is said," remarked the Rev. Harry Anderson, of Partick, at a meeting held in Glasgow at the time of the Declaratory Act controversy, "we must bring the *Confession* up to date, to be adapted to the more enlarged ideas and the living faith of the modern church, by this new Declaratory Act. But in seeking to remodel the *Confession of Faith* we must take care that we are not remodelling the Word of God. For it is the doctrine in the *Confession of Faith* that is hateful to some. We wish progress in sanctified Bible criticism, and constructive, and not destructive, criticism. We wish this Book defended against all attacks, and no cutting and carving of it. Our Free Church had a crown of gold on her head in 1843. There was no hesitancy then with regard to the Church's testimony for Jesus the Prophet, Who speaks in His Word, with all its infallible Truth and Divine authority; for Jesus the Priest, Who is the sin-bearer and curse-bearer, and substitute of His people in making the atonement; and for Jesus the King of Zion and the King of nations. All was then 'fair as the moon' and 'clear as the sun.' But I fear the terrible words are being fulfilled, 'The sun shall go down over the prophets, and the day shall be dark over them'."

As after events proved, this fear was not the misgiving of a timid alarmist but the forecast of a true prophet.

1. *Proceedings of General Assembly of Free Church 1846;* Act 12.
2. J. R. Fleming's *The Church in Scotland, 1875-1929;* p. 18.
3. ibid., pp. 21, 22.
4. *Proceedings of General Assembly of Free Church 1892;* Act 12 anent Confession of Faith.
5. K. Moody Stuart's *Letter to a Friend re the Declaratory Act;* p. 14.
6. J. Kennedy's *Unionism and the Union;* p. 39.

CHAPTER FOURTEEN

UNION NEGOTIATIONS RESUMED

The separation of naturalistic liberalism from the evangelical churches would no doubt greatly diminish the size of the churches. But Gideon's three hundred were more powerful than the thirty-two thousand with which the march against the Midianites began.—Professor J. Gresham Machen.

In 1895 the Free Church General Assembly decided to wait no longer for the resumption of union negotiations with the United Presbyterian Church. Two years later a Union Committee was formed which, with very little delay, began to prepare a plan of Union. While they were at work the advocates of Union were busy up and down the country, especially in the areas where opposition was most to be feared. Church union was to be the panacea for all ecclesiastical ills and disorders! And the Free Church of Scotland was to enter it without change of principle, and without departure from her time-honoured Standards. In May 1898 the General Assembly resolved that a two days' convention should be held under Free Church auspices in Inverness. Held ostensibly for the deepening of spiritual life its obvious purpose was to offset the influence of the Constitutionalists in an area where they had their strongest followings. Dr Alexander Whyte of Edinburgh, the Moderator of the Free Church General Assembly that year, presided, and several representative Free Churchmen, both clerical and lay, took part. With fine diplomacy it was decided that there should be no direct reference to the matters of controversy which were then agitating the Church, and that the addresses should bear on the work of the Free Church in general, with particular reference to evangelism and Foreign Missions. Rev. John McNeil, then at the peak of his popularity as an evangelist, who was one of the speakers, was never the most predictable of men, and for some uneasy moments the platform party must have regretted his presence among them. For Mr McNeil came perilously near to the matters at dispute. Referring to his evangelistic crusades, he disclosed that in his work he found that he would "have to part company with the thing called 'modern criticism'." He knew something of it, for he passed through the College when it was in the air. He thanked God for the steadying influence of the Shorter Catechism, and warned young preachers that "they must never yield any point as to the external security and strength of God's Word. When I was a young and anxious Free Kirker,"* he said, "what helped me more than anything else in coming to Christ and finding Him was this — the Free Kirk then taught that the Bible was right, that the road to Christ lay there. I knew that the Bible was the road, and it was a sure road, and I was bound to find Him. The modern critic tells you no; he puts up a notice at the head of it, 'This road is under repairs.' They have howked it up, and there is no traffic; they always say that they are going to give us a better one, but they haven't done it yet."[1]

In the first Union controversy a Free Church Defence Association had been formed. In 1898 it was revived and, on the eve of Union, it issued a manifesto wherein were set forth the considerations which had led the Constitutionalists to their decision to resist to the utmost of their power a Church Union which it was proposed to achieve by the abandonment, on the Free Church side, of vital and distinctive principles.

"It is established beyond all serious controversy," says the manifesto, "that the Church cannot by a majority of votes, however large, change its Constitution. The majority adopting the change will fall outside of the Church. We have it upon most eminent legal opinion that the changes proposed are at variance with the Constitution of our Church, and that only those who adhere to the Constitution and standards will remain legally entitled to the Church, its name, privileges and property. As trustees for the inheritance bequeathed to us by our fathers, we are bound to invoke the protection of the law on behalf of our Church, and we intend to do so."

There were some who, later, charged the Free Church loyalists with overmuch interest in the property question, but their vindication came from a leading figure on the United Free side. In reply to a question as to why no attempt had been made to compromise with the Free Church before proceeding to legal action, C. J. Guthrie, one of the principal legal advisers of the United Free Church, replied, "The idea of compromise does injustice to the Free Church leaders. I believe their first concern was not with the loaves and fishes. What they wanted, and were determined to have, was a finding by the law courts that they represented the Free Church of 1843, and that we did not. If so, evidently the real subject of dispute between us was one on which there could be no compromise."[2]

* In 1891, John McNeil agreed to the proposal of Mr J. Campbell White (afterwards Lord Overtoun), that he should leave the local pastorate and go out as an itinerant evangelist, supported, in the main, by Mr White. At times, he returned for short periods to congregational work under different auspices. But in a series of autobiographical articles which he contributed to the Scots Observer after his retirement he affirmed his lifelong attachment to the teaching of the Church of his youth and early ministry. Writing as an old campaigner who was ending his warfare, he declared that he gave up his sword to the Free Church of Scotland.

In those words Lord Guthrie* (as he later became), sets the matter at issue in correct perspective. The name and the Constitution of the Free Church of Scotland were at stake, and the loyalists who remained in the Free Church after the secession of 1893 were determined to safeguard and retain the heritage bequeathed to posterity by the Disruption Fathers. The Declaratory Act legislation, they protested, was incompetent. The ministers and elders of the Church held their office in virtue of their ordination pledges which bound them to the *Westminster Confession* as the principal subordinate standard of the Church. In the General Assembly their commission bound them ". . . there to consult, vote and determine in all matters that come before them to the glory of God and the good of His Church according to the Word of God, the Confession of Faith, and agreeable to the constitution of this Church, as they will be answerable. . . ." How such a commission could be taken as conferring upon the holders the liberty to change the Church's relation to the *Confession,* and indeed, to her own Constitution, is beyond ordinary comprehension. There was no enactment governing the Constitution which allowed change by a majority vote, or which gave power to disinherit the minority who were opposed to such a change. Rev. D. M. Macalister, one of the minority in 1900, lays down as a general proposition, "that no mere majority, however large, can alter the terms of the bond into which this Church entered with me and I with it . . . without my consent; neither, even if the terms were unaltered, can I be handed over to a new Church whether I will or not."[3]

Another important fact has to be kept in mind, viz. that even if it had been competent for the Free Church to change her Constitution, so long as the ordination vows taken by her office-bearers, and the formula signed at their induction to office, remained unchanged, the alterations in the Constitution would remain without effect. For these reasons the supporters of the Constitutional position continued the fight from within, consistently opposing the revisionary legislation step by step, and dissenting from the findings of the General Assembly when their amendments were defeated, thus clearing themselves from complicity in the unconstitutional legislation that was passed. When eventually the change was made in the Questions and Formula that made the Declaratory Act of 1892 operative, the minority claimed that the majority were no longer in direct continuity with the Free Church of 1843 but had, in fact, formed a new denomination. Loudly derided at the time, they had their

*In a note made during the first hearing in the House of Lords, Guthrie makes the admission, "I have never believed in the legal soundness of our case as Haldane has done and does." (Orr's *Life of Lord Guthrie;* p. 138).

full vindication when the supreme legislature in the land pronounced upon their appeal in 1904.

As the months passed, the faith and courage of the Constitutionalists were severely tested by regrettable defections from their ranks. That of Rev. Murdoch MacAskill of Dingwall was probably the sorest blow of all. Mr MacAskill had been an outspoken critic of the Declaratory Act manoeuvre in earlier days and had repeatedly asserted his opposition to any move for union which would have the effect of weakening in any way the constitutional framework of the Free Church of Scotland. But as the day of reckoning drew near it became clear that he was having second thoughts. It is one thing to plan courageously; it is quite another to carry the plan into effect. So in the 1897 General Assembly, when Dr Rainy moved for action on the basis of the Union Committee's Report, Mr MacAskill proposed an addition to Rainy's motion which, if accepted, would leave him free to pass over to the Unionist side, an action which, on the evidence of his supporting speech, he was now ready to take. With studied care he elaborated the large measure of agreement which subsisted between the uniting bodies. Just one thing required to be cleared up, and it was with this one matter that his amendment dealt. Let it be affirmed that the doctrine of the *Westminster Confession* relating to the powers and duties of the Civil Magistrate would continue to be binding on the ministers and elders of the Church, subject to the explanatory statement given in Act XII, 1846, and all would be well!

Voices were raised in support of Mr MacAskill's proposal, and Dr Rainy was urged to accept it. But he refused, knowing full well that such an addendum would give the United Presbyterians second thoughts about uniting with the Free Church. Before the vote was taken, however, Dr Rainy indicated that if Mr MacAskill's motion carried, he would have a proposal to make concerning it that, he thought, might satisfy Mr MacAskill and his supporters. A subservient Assembly took the hint dropped by its recognised master of strategy and carried Mr MacAskill's motion, whereupon Principal Rainy proposed that it should be forwarded to the Union Committee for their consideration as a statement "expressing reasonable anxieties of brethren in the Assembly on the points referred to." That was all; but Mr MacAskill expressed his concurrence. Thereafter he was appointed a member of the Union Committee and became an ardent advocate of the Union which he had previously opposed.

Dr George Reith, in his *Reminiscences of the United Free Church General Assembly,* cites Dr Rainy's treatment of Mr MacAskill as an instance of Rainy's adroitness in dealing with awkward opponents. "Rainy . . ." he writes, "deftly manoeuvred

Mr Murdo MacAskill of Dingwall . . . into a position where he not only did not oppose, but actually seconded the Principal's motion." And he adds a reminiscence regarding two Aberdeenshire elders who, in an interval, were washing their hands at adjoining basins in the lavatory. "Said one to the other: 'Ay, he's a graun' man, that Principal Rainy! Heard ye ever the like o' the wye he got roon' that man MacAskill?' 'Ay,' replied the other, 'it wis fine. An' yet he's got nae mair expression on's face nor a pigeon hiz'."[4]

Clever, perhaps; but it was incidents like this that often led the outside world (as Reith for all his admiration of Rainy acknowledges), to regard Rainy as "an astute and unscrupulous ecclesiastical Machiavelli."

Another desertion from the Constitutionalists was led by Rev. R. G. MacIntyre of Maxwelltown, who also had taken part in Presbytery and Assembly debates on the Union question. In association with some like-minded friends he now submitted a Declaration setting forth the conditions under which they were now prepared to desist from opposing the proposed basis of Union. Professing to hold unyieldingly to the Establishment Principle, they proceeded to an examination of the new Questions and Formula to be used in the United Church. These, they judged, laid no obligations upon them beyond what they had already accepted. They were therefore prepared to enter the Union on the distinct understanding "that no existing principle of the Free Church had been or was proposed to be renounced, and that no new principle was to be imposed upon the Church or upon the United Church." Mr MacIntyre moved that the Assembly should receive the Declaration and order it to be engrossed in the minutes.

But Mr MacIntyre and his friends had to be content with much less than they had desired. Dr Rainy expressed his willingness to accept the Declaration as a statement of individual views held by certain members of the Church, but not as a public utterance of the mind of the Church. If the supporters of the Declaration would agree to this interpretation of it he would be willing to receive it as an addition to his own motion expressing approval of the Union Committee's Report, and would have it engrossed in the minutes. The signatories of the Declaration had intended that official authority should be given to their statement, but Rainy made it quite clear that its only chance of survival was in the ineffective form which he proposed for it.

MacIntyre and his supporters signified their acceptance of the Principal's proposal, and gerrymandering politics carried the plan for Union a stage farther.

It says much for the courage and conviction of the small band of Constitutionalists who now remained that, at a conference held at Achnasheen, in the wilds of Ross-shire, they reaffirmed their determination, "by the grace of God and under the guidance of His Holy Spirit, to maintain inviolate the Free Church of Scotland and its testimony, as contained in the *Claim, Declaration and Protest* of 1842, and *Protest* of 1843, wherein the Headship of Christ over the Nation, as well as over His own Church, is fully set forth, and the duty of the National recognition and support of religion. Further (they proceeded) we declare it to be our duty to endeavour to preserve the property of the Free Church for the purposes for which it was contributed, and for this purpose, to prevent by all lawful means which may be open to us the alienation of its funds and property for the propagation of principles contrary to those embodied in the Standards and Constitution of the Church of Scotland — Free."[5]

In deciding upon this the Constitutionalists were well aware that they were making their stand in a Scotland that had changed greatly since Disruption times. The neo-rationalism of the popular pulpit had lowered the spiritual tone of Scottish national life. Increasing material prosperity was engrossing the thoughts of the people to the neglect of theological and ecclesiastical questions. Whatever the "experts" said would command the support of the majority, and the most vocal of the "experts" were almost without exception on the side of theological change and union at any price. There would be no popular acclaim for the defenders of the Church's Constitution and testimony as there had been for the Evangelicals of 1843. The storm of abuse which broke upon them caused them no surprise, nor did it daunt them. They had counted the cost. They were concerned with principle, not with popularity.

The opposition of the minority group to the proposals of the Union Committee was expressed in the General Assembly of May 1900 in a motion by the Rev. Angus Galbraith of Lochalsh, which disapproved the Committee's recommendations on the ground that they did not conserve the distinctive principles of the Free Church of Scotland. Mr Galbraith had adhibited his signature to the dissent of the minority who had opposed Union with the United Presbyterians in 1872 and he referred to that incident in moving opposition to the proposed Union of 1900. "I stand now on the same ground as I stood then," he said. . . . "I have endeavoured hitherto to follow the teaching I received in the Free Church, and I am satisfied that that teaching was in accordance with the Word of God. I have just one end in view, and that is to maintain the Free Church and her distinctive principles. It is because we think these principles are not fully conserved that we are constrained to take up this attitude to the proposed Union. I am not an anti-Unionist, but even Union I will not have at the expense of what I consider any part of Divine truth."[5]

But Dr Rainy's motion, approving the Union Committee's Report, was carried overwhelmingly. In accordance therewith, an overture embodying the Committee's proposals regarding the various matters involved in the proposed Union was sent down to the Presbyteries, with the instruction that their decisions should be sent in by 17th October next. A special meeting of Commission of Assembly was held on 24th October, with powers to dispose of all matters requiring attention in preparation for the Assembly which was due to meet on 30th October.

One of the items which came before the Commission was a document which came to be known as the *Mackenzie Declaration*.

In the Highland areas where there was considerable support for the Constitutionalist position, the Unionists had been loudly proclaiming their unswerving loyalty to the Principles of the Free Church of Scotland, and had been giving the assurance that nothing distinctively Free Church would be sacrificed by entering into union with the United Presbyterians. The United Free Church which was to be brought into being would be simply an enlargement of the Free Church of Scotland.

To put the matter to the test, an overture was sent to the General Assembly by the Free Presbytery of Inverness craving that the following Declaration be adopted by the Assembly: "That the Free Church, in entering into this Union, asserts her adherence to her distinctive principles relative to the Headship of Christ over the nations, as these are set forth in the Confession of Faith, the Claim, Declaration and Protest of 1842, the Protest of 1843, Act of 1846 on 'Questions and Formula', and Act and Declaration 'anent the Standards of 1851', and that, notwithstanding the altered questions and formula and preamble to the same, no departure from these Declarations and Acts, or any change in the doctrines of grace, as hitherto understood and received, is intended."[7]

Now, it may be validly objected that such a Declaration, coming so late in the day, could not possibly alter the basis of Union already agreed upon; but, at least, it had the effect of revealing the utter wrongness of the claim that the Free Church Unionists would be carrying the distinctive testimony of the Free Church with them into the Union. Even the legerdemain of Principal Rainy proved inadequate on this occasion. He indeed persuaded the Commission of Assembly to accept the Declaration, but subject to a preamble which evacuated it of all significance. For the Declaration was accepted "without prejudice to the authority of other Acts of Assembly not hereinafter recited," and with the recognition that "the negotiations for Union have been expressly conducted on the footing that neither of the Churches require to relinquish any principle it has previously maintained."

Gestures of this kind had proved effective in winning over R. G. MacIntyre and Murdoch MacAskill, and it may well be that Dr Rainy thought that by similar tactics he could win over the Rev. Murdoch Mackenzie of Inverness, whose name was specially linked with the Declaration. So far, he had not openly committed himself to either side, and it was well known, as his wife admits in her memoir of him, that "he dreaded the loss of fellowship; the loss of the larger current of church life in which his soul delighted." To win him over to the Unionist side would be a major triumph; for as well as having a large and influential congregation in Inverness he had a considerable following all over the Highland area. Would he be satisfied with the Commission's treatment of the Declaration?

Dr Rainy had to wait until the meeting of Assembly for the answer.

When the Assembly met on 30th October it was Dr Rainy who moved the adoption of the overture anent the Uniting Act. There had been a petition signed by 501 elders asking for delay until the Kirk Sessions had been given the opportunity to consider and discuss the whole basis of union and form their judgment upon it, but Dr Rainy had swept it aside with a motion which affirmed that the Assembly "was satisfied that the Union was in accordance with the wishes of the vast majority of the office-bearers and members." His speech supporting the Uniting Act matched the importance of the occasion and displayed all the adroitness of the experienced politician. There was an oblique reference to the men who had deserted the ranks of the Constitutionalists and joined the Unionists, and an implied invitation to others to follow their example. "He would be a wise and patriotic man who disregarded misconstruction and party passion if he was persuaded that in the interest of the cause of Christ, after opposing Union, he made the best of it."

It was the Rev. C. A. Bannatyne of Coulter (later Professor Bannatyne of the Free Church College), who moved the amendment to Principal Rainy's motion. The motion began by "fully recognising the duty of, as well as the many benefits to be derived from, all such closer union with other branches of the Presbyterian Church of Scotland as may be lawfully and consistently entered upon," and went on to assert the propriety of engaging in "such hearty and cordial co-operation as does not involve sacrifice of any vital principle, with all other branches of the Christian Church in every good work." At the same time, it "places upon record its conviction that no true or abiding benefit to the cause of religion can result from any union the terms of which involve, on the part of any Church entering into it, unfaithfulness to the views of truth on matters of faith and doctrine revealed and adopted by such Church as its distinctive testimony, in the truth of which it professes, as at the time of such proposed union, still to believe; and, in particular, it places on record its sense that, so far as the Free Church of Scotland is concerned, no terms of union can be accepted as satisfactory which fail to make clear, adequate, specific, and unequivocal provision for the maintaining in their entirety the constitution of the Free Church of Scotland, and those distinctive views of truth, in regard to matters of faith and doctrine, which, at her separation from the Establishment in 1843, were deliberately adopted, and have been, and still are, maintained as the distinctive testimony of the Church, and especially for maintaining inviolate (1) the whole superior and secondary standards of the Church in their entirety, and (2) the special testimony of the Church in regard to the right and duty of the civil magistrate to maintain and support an establishment of religion, in accordance with God's Word, as the same is contained and set forth in the *Claim, Declaration, and Protest by Commissioners to the Assembly, forming Act 19 of 1842,* the *Protest by Commissioners to the Assembly, forming Act 1 of 1843,* and the other Acts confirming the same; and having fully considered the terms of the Act of Union with the United Presbyterian Church now reported upon, declines to pass the said Act and relative declarations in respect they do not contain provisions as aforesaid."[8]

In seconding Mr Bannatyne's motion, Mr Archibald MacNeilage took the opportunity of expressing gratitude to Dr Rainy for his efforts to understand the position of the minority and, as he put it, "to secure for us a place in the Church which comes into being tomorrow." "I am not saying anything out of place," he continued, "when I ask the Principal to believe regarding those of us who today stand at the parting of the ways, and know we are going to part if the motion is carried, that it is not because we have any disregard for the welfare of religion in Scotland that we feel ourselves today in the position in which we stand."

He had yet to learn, said Mr MacNeilage "that the history of the United Presbyterian Church was the testimony of the Free Church. It was not so, and, as far as he had observed, no United Presbyterian had ever said it was. They (the anti-unionists), had been asked where they were going. As he understood it, they were not going anywhere. They were Free Churchmen, and they were just remaining Free Churchmen."

The amendment, of course, was lost by an overwhelming majority, but it is of lasting interest as setting forth the position of its supporters in regard to the reunion of Scottish Presbyterianism, as well as to ecclesiastical co-operation in its wider aspects.

When the Rev. Murdo Mackenzie of Inverness was seen making for the platform there was a perceptible quickening of interest in the Assembly. Dr Rainy had given the hint. Was Mr Mackenzie about to announce his acceptance?

The Assembly was not long left in suspense. Mr Mackenzie had not been present at the Commission which had dealt with the Declaration. He had been ill, and was not yet fully recovered; but his decision regarding the Declaration could not be delayed any longer, and he had come to announce it personally. He was there, he said, "to carry out his own convictions, which were not known, he might say, to any member of the Assembly, so far as he was aware. He was one of those who did not take part in any agitation on the one side or the other, but one of those who endeavoured to the best of his ability to keep down agitation. He had seen the calamity that was impending. He had seen what was to happen in his own native Highlands, and the disastrous and dire results that would flow from this Union if it took place, and, therefore, he had done everything in his power, in concert with two or three brethren, to devise ways and means by which this dire calamity could be averted. The history of their attempt was well known to the House. They had thought that if they got a declaration that would declare to the whole country that the Free Church was going into this Union carrying all her own distinctive principles — that that would go very far to bring brethren to see face to face," The Declaration, he continued, "found its way to the last Commission, but with what result? — with this result, that looking upon it in the light of Principal Rainy's speech, as also of his preamble, this Declaration meant nothing for them. It had no bearing on the basis of Union. Their opposition was not to the Union, but to the basis of Union—and when this Declaration did not in the least affect the basis of Union, where did they stand? . . . One of the Acts which was to be carried out by declaration of the Church was the Declaratory Act. The Declaratory Act would affect the distinctive principles of the Free Church, and their declaration would be brought under the Act as well as other Acts. . . . He felt very much on the subject, and hence his appearance there against the advice of the doctor. At the same time he could not allow the opportunity to pass without declaring himself on the side of the principles of the Free Church in their entirety, and that he was prepared to stand by those principles as he had been trained to them from his youth, and by men who had now gone to their everlasting rest."[9]

Dr Rainy's disappointment over the failure to win Mr Mackenzie and his supporters was understandable, but the bitterness of his rejoinder was out of character, and it gave offence even to some of his own supporters. "His face was white with passion," recalls one who was present in the Assembly at the time, "and his voice quivered with bitter and scornful feeling as he charged Mr Mackenzie with insincerity in his relation to the whole proposal, and taunted him with having given a singularly confused impression of the whole business."

There was a reference to the incident some years later when Sir William Robertson Nicoll, writing on the death of Dr Black, of Inverness, recalled that his last meeting with him was at the General Assembly that decided for Union. "Principal Rainy," he says, "had made a severe comment on Mr Mackenzie, Inverness. Dr Black turned round to me and said, 'That is quite wrong — quite unjust. Mackenzie has been perfectly straight throughout'."[10]

Mr Mackenzie's last-minute decision to take his stand with the defenders of the Free Church Constitution had a consolidating effect upon the Free Church loyalists in the Highlands of Scotland; and for the remaining thirteen years of his ministry he held his large congregation in the Free North Church, and, to the utmost of his failing strength, gave valiant service to the Free Church in the years of its recovery from the disastrous set-back of 1900.

1. *Report of Convention at Inverness,* 1898; p. 25.
2. R. L. Orr, *Lord Guthrie; A Memoir;* p. 146.
3. D. M. Macalister, *Union Question;* p. 3.
4. G. M. Reith, *Reminiscences of the United Free Church General Assembly;* p. 14.
5. Stewart and Cameron, *Free Church of Scotland 1843-1910;* p. 98.
6. J. Galbraith, *Sermons and Biography of Rev. Angus Galbraith;* p. 19.
7. J. B. Orr, *Scotch Church Crisis;* p. 31.
8. *Proceedings of Free Church General Assembly,* 1900.
9. E. S. Mackenzie, *Memoir of Rev. Murdo Mackenzie;* p. 212, 213.
10. ibid. p. 214.

CHAPTER FIFTEEN

THE PARTING OF THE WAYS

From a majority of pulpits little is being proclaimed but a superficial moralism, a be-good and do-good gospel that, like the gospel which was casting its spell over the churches of Galatia in the apostolic age, in reality is no gospel at all.—*Professor R. B. Kuyper.*

The defeat of the motion opposing Union in the 1900 May Assembly of the Free Church was, of course, foreseen by the minority and, indeed, prepared against. To the noisy derision of their former brethren they claimed that the majority, by committing themselves to the basis of Union, had put themselves outside the Free Church of Scotland whose Constitution and principles they had violated. When therefore the Assembly voted to adjourn for the day and meet the next day in the Waverley Market in union with the United Presbyterians, the minority sat on to continue the Free Church General Assembly in order to arrange for the new circumstances in which they found themselves. On the pretext that the main Assembly Hall was required for a Committee meeting they were denied the use of it, but, after some difficulty, foregathered in one of the side rooms to attend to their business. There they were opposed by members of the Unionist majority who had followed them, but, despite obstruction, they appointed Rev. C. A. Bannatyne as Moderator, and the Rev. J. Kennedy Cameron of Brodick—who had given outstanding service as Clerk of the Defence Association—as Clerk. They then adjourned to meet again the following day in the Assembly Hall after the Union party had left for the Waverley Market. But in this they were thwarted; for the majority, sensing the embarrassment of leaving the minority in occupancy of any part of the Free Church Assembly Hall when they themselves set out for the Waverley Market,* made a last-minute change in their plans and left from the High Church (now the New College

---

* There was a jarring note at the Waverley Market meeting when it came to the reception of delegates from other Churches. Dr Joseph Parker, of the City Temple, London, in his eagerness to please his audience, went farther than prudence and good taste allowed. The Free Church section of the Assembly had discreetly refrained from an open repudiation of the Establishment Principle, preferring to leave it as an "open question." Parker, a Voluntary himself, and a lover of the dramatic, believing that an emphatic repudiation of the Establishment Principle would gratify the ears of his audience, declared that it was "unbecoming for the Bride of Christ to be the concubine of Caesar." In the circumstances, nothing could have been more inopportune. Dr George Reith tells that Parker was "obviously startled and confused" by the loud murmur of protest that broke out at his words.

Library) instead of making the Assembly Hall their place of gathering as originally intended. When, therefore, the Free Church minority arrived at the Assembly Hall it was to find that the gates had been locked against them, and that two policemen and an insolent janitor were in charge with instructions to keep them out. Their request for admission to their own building was denied them, whereupon they lodged a Notarial Protest against the action of the majority and constituted the General Assembly of the Free Church of Scotland on the street outside the locked gates, thereafter adjourning to meet in Queen Street Hall for the remaining meetings of their Assembly.

That experience outside the Assembly Hall on the drizzly morning of 31st October 1900 was a plain indication to them of the intentions of their former brethren. As they had excluded them from their usual place of assembly, so they purposed excluding them from participation in any part of the patrimony of the Free Church of Scotland. For it was not until the House of Lords Appeal showed signs of turning in favour of the remanent Free Church that Dr Rainy and his followers offered to place £50,000 at the disposal of the minority for its work and witness. And even then an insult was attached to the offer, for it was specifically laid down that, as a condition of the award, the recipients must withdraw their appeal to the Lords. Furthermore, it was stated that the sum offered was not to be drawn from the trust funds of the Church; it was to be specially raised. Thus the Free Church appellants were to be treated as sturdy beggars who must be silenced somehow, and not as members of the Free Church household who had a clear right to participate in the family inheritance. A reference to this offer was made at the time by *The Scotsman*. It read, "An attempt was made to buy the consciences of the minority by a bribe of £50,000. In history there will not be found many parallels to this proposal. To their honour, it has to be recorded that the few who had refused to bow the knee to Baal of Union refused the bribe."[1]

The writer, it may be worth adding, did not belong to either party in the case.

A picture of the Queen Street Hall Assembly survives, and if ever a product of the photographer's art represented a forlorn hope that one appeared to do so. The curving seats were sparsely occupied. The Commissioners, for the most part, were elderly men. The Moderator had already spent many years in the service of the Church and was showing clear signs of having borne the burden and heat of the day. Rainy's gibe that they were "playing at Free Church" seemed justified, and his allocation to them of a denominational existence of five years seemed not ungenerous. The prospects were bleak indeed, and it was clearly the intention

108

of the United Free Church that they should become bleaker still, for not only did the ministers who had entered the Union claim possession of churches and manses—even where a mere fraction of the congregations had followed them—but the rights of possession of those who had continued the Free Church were challenged in a letter sent to them by the Law Agents of the United Free Church. The following paragraph is a quotation from the letter referred to:

"Whilst our clients do not propose at present to take legal proceedings to recover possession of the church from you, we are requested to state that their not doing so in the meantime is only for the sake of peace, and that it is in no way to be held as acquiescence in your possession of the church and other property, nor to prejudice the right of the United Free Church of Scotland to the same."[2]

Petty exhibitions of ill-will became common. Boyd-Orr lists some of them. "Rev. Mr Noble, of Lairg, had an annuity of £100 as Free Church minister of the parish. He held to the Free Church, and attempts to raise a U.F. congregation failed, so that he was undoubtedly the Free Church minister, but Principal Rainy was one of the trustees of the fund which was held by the Church, and in 1901 the annuity was stopped. Mr Mackay, of Contin, a schoolmaster, who received an annuity from the funds of the Church for work done in the Free Church schools before 1872, used his influence for the Free Church. His annuity was stopped. The only way he could have it continued was by entering the Union. Mr Mackay did without the annuity. Mr Farquhar Matheson, of Lochalsh, a bed-ridden Catechist, who in his day had served the Church well, declared for the Free Church. His name was immediately scored off from those who received money from the central funds. . . . Mr Auld, of Olrig, was forced to retire in 1901 through age and infirmity, and was entitled to receive £80 a year from the Aged and Infirm Ministers' Fund, into which his congregation had been paying all along. He received nothing, and at his death £320 was legally due to him."

The situation was comparable, in some respects, with that in which the Free Church of Scotland, in 1843, began her separate existence. Yet there was a very important difference in the respect that whereas in 1843 the outgoing ministers, because they were leaving the Establishment, voluntarily relinquished all the benefits which went with State connection, and were concerned only with the maintenance of the Church's Constitution; in 1900 the section of the Free Church which held loyally to the Church's principles and testimony were threatened with dispossession by the section which had tampered with the Church's Constitution for the sake of effecting a union with a denomination which was

109

constitutionally and doctrinally different—and, to their honour made no secret about it! For their loyalty to ordination vows which bound them to the Standards of the Free Church of Scotland the Free Church minority were judged to have "no right or title to the property of the said Church or any part thereof."

Dr Rainy's reference to the Free Church, in the Assembly of 1903, as "those who had lapsed," strengthened the determination of the former Free Church ministers who had entered the Union to treat them in precisely that character, and unseemly squabbles over the occupancy of buildings became common.

The scene of the most widely publicised of these was the district of Ness in the north of the Island of Lewis. Only a relatively small section of the large congregation there had followed their minister into the Union. The Free Church section approached the minister to discuss arrangements with him whereby they also might have the use of the Church building for public worship; but the request was refused. Angered by what they regarded as an utterly unjustifiable refusal, the Free Church party took forcible possession, whereupon the minister secured an interim interdict against them from the Sheriff-Substitute at Stornoway. Acting upon the principle that "possession is eleven points in the law" the men of Ness decided to ignore the interdict, whereupon Lord Balfour of Burleigh, then Secretary for Scotland, and C. J. Guthrie, then Sheriff for the county, advised that a gun-boat, carrying a force of around 100 policemen drawn from over a wide area, be sent to Ness, under cover of darkness, to enforce respect for the law, At the same time a regiment of soldiers was held in readiness at Fort George to proceed to Lewis at the shortest notice if required. The plan was to land the policemen at Port of Ness under cover of the ship's guns in the event of resistance.

Meanwhile information regarding the planned expedition was privately given to the Assembly Clerk of the Free Church, Rev. J. Kennedy Cameron. Apprehensive of the dire consequences of such an unwise move, Mr Cameron obtained permission from the authorities concerned to proceed at once to Lewis in an endeavour to prevent further disorder.

Arriving at Ness, Mr Cameron gathered the dissidents together and explained to them the unwisdom of what they had done. Their strife was no longer with the United Free Church but with the law of the land, and perhaps even with the armed forces of the kingdom. He advised them not to make any show of resistance to the representatives of the law when they came, but to let them come and go peaceably.

Returning to the mainland, Mr Cameron was able to intercept the police force who were on their way to join the gun-boat, and to give them his views on the situation which awaited them in Lewis. The result was gratifying. "All that this formidable array of police got to do," concludes Mr Cameron, "after amusing the sailors on board the ship with their helplessness produced by the movements of the Minch, was to return home after a characteristically kind reception by the people of the Island."[3]

R. L. Orr, in his *Life of Lord Guthrie,* passes lightly over Guthrie's part in sending the gun-boat. He quotes from a letter written by Guthrie at the time, in which he says, "A wire from Lord Balfour that he is endeavouring to arrange for a gun-boat for Saturday week in accordance with my request. . . . If a military expedition is necessary I shall go. But if we get a gun-boat and eighty police, as proposed . . . this may settle the business and make the military unnecessary." Orr adds, "Then the gunboat and the eighty police fade from the scene and the Sheriff is presumably left in peace."

The Chief Constable of the County in his report of the incident gratefully acknowledged the helpful restraint of the Free Church in what might have been a very ugly situation.

The policy of the United Free Church in dealing with the Free Church minority was one of complete denominational extermination. All the invested funds of the Church were placed in the hands of new Trustees, some of whom were former United Presbyterians, to be held and administered in behoof of the United Free Church. Congregations who declined to enter the Union were held (to quote from the pleadings of the United Free Church), to have "separated and cut themselves off from the said Church" (i.e. the Free Church of Scotland), and, by so doing, to have "lost and forfeited all their rights and privileges as members thereof."

It was a situation in which the intervention of the law was clearly called for, and in December 1900 the famous law-case listed as *Bannatyne* versus *Overtoun* was begun. The Free Church leaders were advised in advance as to the probable outcome of their action in the Scottish Courts. The feeling against them was intense, and it was almost too much to expect that in the prevailing atmosphere the Scottish law Lords should be proof against popular prejudice. To say this is is not to impugn their judicial integrity but merely to recognise that, even in the best and most competent of men, there can be a tendency to judge according to expedient rather than by strict legal principle.

The first hearing of the case was before Lord Low in the Court of Session. The Free Church pursuers asked that it be "found and declared . . . that the properties and money vested as at 30th October 1900 in Lord Overtoun and others as trustees were held by them for behoof of the Free Church, and could not lawfully be

111

diverted to the use of any other association, or at least of any other association not maintaining the whole principles embodied in the constitution of the said Free Church without the consent of the said Church, or at least the unanimous assent of the members of its Assembly."

The United Free Church, they averred, had not preserved intact "the whole principles fundamental in the constitution of the Free Church." They had abandoned the Establishment Principle, a principle firmly embedded in the constitution of the Free Church. Furthermore, by the Declaratory Act of 1892, now made fully operative 'by the Act of Union and the changes in formula and ordination vows, they had altered their relation to the *Westminster Confession of Faith,* the principal subordinate standard of the Church. They therefore had "no right, title, or interest in any part of the said lands, property, or funds," and the trustees should denude themselves of these in favour of trustees appointed by the Free Church of Scotland.

Against this view the United Free Church maintained that the section of the Free Church which had entered the Union had done so without any change of principle. In their opinion, the Establishment Principle was not a fundamental principle in the constitution of the Free Church of Scotland, and it was quite competent for them to regard it as an open question. As touching the alleged alteration of relationship to the *Confession,* they held that in sending down the Declaratory Act to the Presbyteries of the Church under the Barrier Act procedure they had acted in accordance with the Constitution, and the returns from Presbyteries had showed convincingly that the mind of the Free Church was for union. Furthermore, with regard to property, they based their claim on the Model Trust Deed of 1844 in terms of which the buildings belonging to congregations should be held.

This Deed provided that every place of worship held in connection with the Free Church should be "used as and for a place of worship by a congregation of the . . . body of Christians called the Free Church of Scotland, or of any united body of Christians composed of them and of such other body or bodies of Christians as the said Free Church of Scotland may at any time hereafter associate with themselves under the foresaid name of the Free Church of Scotland, or under whatever name or designation they may assume."

Lord Low's judgment in favour of the United Free Church was not unexpected by the pursuers. He regarded the passing of the Declaratory Act of 1892 as a legitimate exercise of the powers inherent in the General Assembly inasmuch as the procedure prescribed in the Barrier Act had been followed. In this, however, he revealed a complete misapprehension of the purpose of the

Barrier Act. Passed in 1697, this Act was designed to prevent "any sudden alteration, or innovation, or other prejudice to the Church in either doctrine or worship, or discipline, or government thereof." Its purpose was regulative and restrictive. It protected the Constitution of the Church from the damage that hasty and immature legislation might inflict by putting it beyond the power of any single Assembly to introduce changes that might be at variance with the standards and principles of the Church. The Church's office-bearers met in Presbytery, Synod or General Assembly, being pledged to the *Westminster Confession,* could not competently change the Constitution of the Church, no matter the strength of their majority, nor could they unchurch a dissenting minority, no matter how small it might be, who were resolved to abide by the Constitution to which they had solemnly pledged themselves.

Regarding the Establishment Principle, while Lord Low recognised that the Free Church had come out from the Establishment still adhering to the Establishment Principle, he did not regard that principle so fundamental to the Constitution of the Free Church that it might not be held as an "open question," as indeed the uniting parties had agreed to do in 1900. But his judgment, though unfavourable to the Free Church, had certain aspects that were in line with their pleadings. For example, he dismissed the claim, put forward by the United Free Church, that the General Assembly had inherent powers that were virtually unlimited. The Free Church, he allowed, had a definite Constitution embodying certain specific articles of belief, the abandonment of which would mean the termination of its own existence. The maintaining of the Church's identity depended on her continued maintenance of these essential principles. But the alterations which the United Free Church had made were not, in his view, of so fundamental a character as to impinge upon the Church's constitution.

Undaunted by their failure before the Lord Ordinary the Free Church pursuers carried their case to the Second Division of the Court of Session, where it was heard by Lord Kingsburgh, Lord Young and Lord Trayner. The result again was defeat for the Free Church. Lord Kingsburgh relegated the Establishment Principle to a subordinate place in the Church's Constitution. It was not a fundamental principle. The Church could dispense with it and yet be able to perform all her functions. Like Lord Low he laid stress on the Barrier Act, a measure which, he held, recognised in the Church, acting through her General Assembly, an almost unrestricted power of change. Referring to the Model Trust Deed, he inclined to the view that if the ministers of the Church who had declined to participate in the Union had

113

represented one-third or more of the entire ministry, then, in cases where a dissenting minister was supported by the majority of his congregation, they would have been entitled to retain the church-buildings in which they worshipped. But the Free Church minority was too small, in his judgment, to make good any such claim. So he decided against them.

Lord Young went even farther in his conclusions. He found no rule of law to prevent non-established Churches from abandoning or modifying their distinctive principles, if they so desired, and carrying their property with them through whatever credal alterations they might, from time to time, make. Having an inherent right to effect doctrinal changes, they were not answerable under civil law in the matter of their trust funds and property.

Lord Trayner took the view that the section of the Free Church which had entered into union with the United Presbyterians had done so without making any essential change in doctrine. With regard to the Establishment Principle, he agreed that the pro-Union party in the Free Church had indeed changed from their pre-1900 attitude, but this change had not affected anything that he regarded as an essential in the Church's constitution. The Establishment Principle related to polity and government; not to faith and doctrine. The Church, therefore, "had the power to abandon that principle, and, to that extent, to alter its Constitution."

Of the three pronouncements in the Second Division of the Court of Session that of Lord Young was the most radical, but the three concurred in favouring the United Free Church. The irrelevancies and inaccuracies which came to light in these judgments have been discerningly pin-pointed by Dr Alexander Stewart and Dr J. Kennedy Cameron in their book *The Free Church of Scotland; 1843-1910,* and by J. B. Orr (later Lord Boyd-Orr), in the survey which he makes of the case in his book *Scotch Church Crisis.* It would be to little purpose therefore to cover this ground again, especially since the voluminous record of the whole case may be consulted in *The Free Church of Scotland Appeals,* competently edited by Robert Low Orr.

Not surprisingly, the United Free Church expected that the dismissal of the Free Church appeal by the Second Division of the Court of Session would mark the end of the litigation, if for no other reason than that the financial resources of the Free Church were by this time in such depleted condition as to make an appeal to the House of Lords impossible. But the worsted contestants found generous helpers in their time of need, and their legal advisers were confident that in the calmer atmosphere, and by the more leisurely procedure of the Supreme Court their clients would obtain the judgment which the lower courts had denied them. Accordingly, they again appealed, and the case opened in the House of Lords on 24th November 1903, and was argued during eight sittings extending over two weeks. There was a bench of six judges including Lord Halsbury, the Lord Chancellor. But before judgment could be delivered, Lord Shand, one of the judges, died suddenly, and it was decided to re-hear the case, adding to the five surviving judges Lord James of Hereford, and Lord Alverstone. All of these were men of outstanding eminence and might be depended upon to bring the highest forensic experience and keenest acumen to bear on the task in hand. And the pleaders who represented both contestants at the bar were men of the highest distinction in their chosen profession. Altogether it was a notable tribunal.

Both parties presented anew the arguments which had been pronounced upon in the lower courts, the Free Church maintaining that the Act of Union between the Free Church majority and the United Presbyterians had the effect of turning the Free Church participants in the Union into seceders from the true Free Church. Thus, by their own action, they had forfeited all right and title to the property of the Free Church of Scotland.

As well as abandoning the Establishment Principle they had replaced the well-defined standards of the *Westminster Confession of Faith* by vague and indefinite standards of belief. The Barrier Act, under which the United Free Church had claimed the right to alter its doctrine, gave them no such powers. It did not define the powers of the General Assembly; this was done in the terms of the commission issued to elected members of the Assembly which reminded them that in the discharge of their Assembly duties they were required "to consult, vote, and determine . . . according to the Word of God, the Confession of Faith, and agreeable to the constitution of the Church." Being bound by such a commission, they had no authority to alter the Constitution or qualify the *Confession* in any way.

The United Free Church re-affirmed their former claim that no fundamental doctrine had been changed, and that what changes had been effected were within the lawful powers of the Church to do so. The Free Church, they argued, was now incorporated in the United Free Church, and those who had declined to enter the Union had thereby separated themselves from the Free Church with forfeiture of all right and title to the funds and property of the Free Church of Scotland.

Of the seven judges who heard the appeal, only two—Lord Macnaghten and Lord Lindley—sided with the United Free Church. Lord Macnaghten claimed for the Free Church that, from the beginning of her separate history, she had always

115

possessed the right to revise and amend her formulae of subscription as she might judge necessary. He rejected the view that she was so bound to the *Confession of Faith* that she had "lost hold and touch of the Supreme Standard of her faith."

Now, to set loyalty to Holy Scripture and loyalty to the *Confession of Faith* in opposition to each other in this way was really to stray from the question at issue, for it had never been disputed that the Church had power to revise her subordinate standards if in any place she might find these to be divergent from, or contrary to, the teaching of Holy Scripture. It had been the concern of the Westminster Divines, as it had been of the Scottish Reformers, that their formulations of doctrine should be in closest conformity to the teaching of Holy Scripture, and the same concern ought to be cherished by all who accept such formularies as the confession of their own faith. The principle of *sola Scriptura* is the very quintessence of Reformed theology. The question really at issue was, not is it competent for a Church to change its Constitution, but is it competent and lawful for it to change its Constitution under which it holds certain trusts, and not only claim retention of those trusts but deprive a minority who conscientiously hold to the unchanged Constitution of all participation in the trusts which go with it?

Lord Lindley, the other judge who sided with the United Free Church, held that the Free Church majority had done nothing in their preparations for Union that could be regarded as *ultra vires*. Yet he rejected the view that the powers of the General Assembly to effect changes in her standards and principles are unlimited, but where the limit lies he does not venture to indicate.

The arguments used by the judges who had dismissed the Free Church appeal in the Court of Session, as well as those used by Lords Macnaghten and Lindley, were effectively countered by the five Lords who pronounced in favour of the Free Church appellants in the final hearing. Lord Davey rejected the interpretation which the defenders had placed upon the Barrier Act, and declared it to be, not an enabling Act, but merely an Act governing procedure. He had come to the conclusion, he said, "that it would be contrary to all principle to infer from the provisions of the Barrier Act, unsupported by any evidence, a power in the General Assembly, or the majority, to vary the trusts upon which the property is held, to the prejudice of a dissentient minority." Referring to the Model Trust Deed, he insisted that this Deed could not be regarded as providing that "the majority controlling the Free Church might, by subverting the basis of that Church, divert the trusts of the congregational property." The Deed, it was true, did contemplate that the Free Church might enter into Union with other Churches, but if it was to carry the

116

trusts with it, such unions must be of such a character that they could be made "without detriment to the Free Church." The union which had brought the United Free Church into being was not of that character.

The view advanced by the United Free Church that "the dissenting ministers, by so dissenting, ceased to be ministers of the Free Church, and lost and forfeited all their rights and privileges as members thereof," was described by Lord James of Hereford as somewhat "Draconic." There was nothing within the Barrier Act which gave "any power to alter the identity of the Church." And as for the Model Trust Deed, there was nothing in it that gave "a power to unite so as to bring into existence a Church incapable of identity with the Free Church."

Lord Robertson spoke in like strain, showing the incongruousness of the view of the majority that it was competent "to introduce the United Presbyterians as beneficiaries" under the trusts of the Free Church of Scotland, while at the same time ousting the dissentient minority " from the benefits of the foundation." The lower courts, he said, misled by "an erroneous construction of the Barrier Act, had greatly over-rated the legislative power of the Church." The case which they had built on that Act did not "support the theory that, in giving to the Free Church, the pious founders of the Free Church were knowingly giving to a Church one of whose inherent qualities was that she could alter her essential principles. Neither history nor law," said Lord Robertson, "makes this out."

Turning to the Model Trust Deed, he described it as "a conveyancer's instrument", and held that its clauses regarding Church union applied "only to such unions as were competent to the Free Church, and were probably suggested by such cases as had occurred."

Lord Robertson dissented strongly from the line of argument followed by Lord Young when the case was before the Second Division of the Court of Session. Lord Young's judgment he said, "wholly rested upon the ground, stated in very sweeping terms, that there is nothing to prevent a dissenting Church from abandoning a religious doctrine, however essential and fundamental, and that an *ex facie* absolute property title cannot be limited by reference, not expressed, to 'the essential doctrines and fundamental principles in the Constitution of the Church'."

It was unnecessary, declared Lord Robertson, to say more of this ground of judgment than that it was in flat contradiction of the decision of the House of Lords in the case of *Craigdallie*. This decision laid down the principle that where a division took place within a religious body the destination of its property was determined, not by any consideration of comparative numerical strength, but by adherence to the original Constitution of the body concerned, unless, indeed, the Constitution itself made provision for the alteration by a majority, of its distinctive principles. There was no such provision in the Constitution of the Free Church of Scotland, so that Lord Young's judgment was at complete variance with the law of the land in the matter.

Referring to Lord Kingsburgh's judgment in the Second Division of the Court of Session, Lord Robertson expressed surprise at Kingsburgh's statement that the Reformed Presbyterian Church "certainly did not hold the Establishment Principle." So far was this from being the case he said, "the Reformed Presbyterians were the ecclesiastical heirs of the Covenanters, who held it passionately. . . . Accordingly, the attitude of the Reformed Presbyterians on the Establishment question was exactly analogous to that of the Free Church."

The leading judgment was given by the Lord Chancellor, and was worthy of its distinguished author. The basic question for the Court to decide, he argued, related to the original purpose of the trust in question. What were the views that the founders regarded as important? That, he held, had been made perfectly clear in the Church's Constitution. The Free Church majority who had entered the 1900 Union had abandoned the Establishment Principle as held by the founders of the Free Church, and had departed from the Calvinistic doctrines set forth in the *Confession of Faith*. Comparing the statements of the Declaratory Act of 1892 with those of the *Westminster Confession of Faith* relative to the same subjects, he showed that the theological position of the former was clearly at variance with that of the latter. He allowed "the right of any man or any collection of men, to change their religious beliefs according to their own consciences" but insisted that "when men subscribe money for a particular object, and leave it behind them for the promotion of that object, their successors have no right to change the object endowed," for "there is nothing in calling an associated body a Church that exempts it from the legal obligations of insisting that money given for one purpose shall not be devoted to another."

Examining the transactions which had brought the United Free Church into being, Lord Halsbury claimed that in fact "the so-called Union" was "not a Union of religious belief at all," but was "only a Union of outward organisations, without a real agreement on questions of doctrine."

"It is not," he said, "the case of two associated bodies of Christians in complete harmony as to their doctrine agreeing to share their funds, but two bodies, each agreeing to keep their separate religious views where they differ, agreeing to make their formularies so elastic as to permit persons to accept them

118

according as their respective consciences will permit. Assuming, as I do, that there are differences of belief between them, these differences are not got rid of by their agreeing to say nothing about them, nor are these essentially diverse views avoided by selecting so elastic a formulary as can be accepted by people who differ, and say that they claim their liberty to retain their differences by purporting to join in one Christian Church. It becomes but a colourable Union, and no trust fund devoted to one form of faith can be shared by another communion simply because they say in effect there are some facts of the *Confession* which we will agree not to discuss, and we will make our formularies such that either of us can accept it. Such an agreement would not, in my view, constitute a Church at all, or, to use Sir William Smith's phrase, it would be a Church without a religion. Its formularies would be designed not to be a *Confession of Faith,* but to be a concealment of such part of the faith as constituted an impediment to the Union."

Lord Alverstone, the last to deliver judgment, was equally emphatic in his rejection of the use which the United Free Church had made of the Barrier Act and the Model Trust Deed. It would be "contrary to every rule of law" applicable to the case before them to claim that this Deed "gave the Assembly of the Free Church power by mere Union to divert the funds to a body which did not conform to the fundamental principles of the Free Church."

Referring to the treatment of the minority proposed by the United Free Church, Lord Alverstone pointed out that it was not alleged that they had changed, or departed from, "any fundamental or essential principles of the Free Church," or that they were not "faithfully carrying out the objects of the Protest of the 18th May, 1843." They were being threatened with ejection from their churches and manses "simply on the ground that they decline to become members of the United Free Church." He was unable, he said, "to support a judgment which would deprive the persons, forming a minority, of their rights, simply on the ground that they are unwilling to become members of a body which has not only abandoned the fundamental principles of the Church to which they belong, but supports a principle essentially different from that on which the Church was founded."

Justice in the end prevailed. The spoilers of the Free Church's heritage were required to divest themselves of the trusts unjustly acquired and restore them to their rightful owners.

1. *The Scotsman,* 2nd August 1904.
2. Stewart and Cameron, *Free Church of Scotland 1843-1910;* p. 141.
3. Kennedy Cameron, *Assembly Clerkship;* pp. 22, 23.

CHAPTER SIXTEEN

THE STRUGGLE FOR SURVIVAL

No one will understand the present case unless he receives into his mind the possibility of people valuing separation as a safeguard for doctrines which they hold intensely.—*Lord Robertson.*

As was inevitable, the House of Lords verdict was given a mixed reception in Scotland. It was not altogether unexpected, as the belated offer of £50,000 to the appellants at the last moments as the price of their acquiescence revealed. But the amount offered was a sufficient indication that the United Free representatives who were behind it were thinking in terms of—at the worst—a Pyrrhic victory for their opponents. It does not appear to have occurred to them, even in their bleakest moments, that they would be held to have forfeited the name of the Free Church of Scotland and all that it entailed. Dr George Reith, in his *Reminiscences of the United Free Church General Assembly,* reconstructs the situation for us, and helps us to assess it from the United Free side. "The disaster was staggering and shattering," he writes. "Despite the apprehensions raised in the minds of many by the proposals of compromise made at last Assembly, no one seemed to be greatly troubled as to the issue of the case. The worst we expected—I speak for the rank and file—was that even though the House of Lords should decide in favour of the appellants on some technical point, it would lay down some principle for a reasonable and equitable division of the property between the litigants, which, though it might entail the loss of much that we valued, would not seriously hamper the Church's activities." But when Dr Reith "marvels at the extraordinary calmness, patience and resolute courage" with which the defeated litigants faced the crisis, one can only marvel at his capacity for wonder! Contemporary records, less partisan in character, show a very different picture. There was an immediate outcry by the leaders of the worsted majority against the august tribunal which had issued a judgment so inept and unjust! "They had been the means," so Dr Reith says, "of bringing the whole Empire, and many beyond it, into cordial agreement with Mr Bumble's zoological classification of the law."[1] Of course, Dr Reith exempts from this withering criticism the two judges who had favoured the United Free pleadings. They alone come back from the fray without a blot on their escutcheons!

120

Dr Reith, however, rather spoils his picture of a calm and patient Church courageously facing the crisis which this shattering reverse had brought upon her when he records that "public meetings were held all over the country, at which the surprise and indignation of the Church at the legal outrage, and its determination to be free at all costs, were the leading notes. . . ."

Such meetings as Dr Reith describes were not only the natural reaction of men who had sustained a public humiliation, but part of a considered policy of rehabilitation and recovery. He recalls that "no responsible leader" to his knowledge, "advocated a return to the *status quo ante bellum* with a view to the retention of the property." The truth is, of course, that they could not have done so without a complete loss of face and the forfeiture of the people's confidence. It would have meant the acceptance of the House of Lords judgment with all its implications—that they had been misled and had misled others; that, in fact, there had been no union between the Free Church of Scotland and the United Presbyterians; that the majority who had seceded from the Free Church for the purpose of union with the United Presbyterians had taken with them a name and property to which they were not entitled; and that they had been less than ingenuous when they had assured the people up and down the country that they were entering the Union with the full testimony of the Free Church. To go back would have meant sackcloth and ashes; and the garb of penitence did not match the prevailing mood. It would be better, they decided, to brazen their way out of the impasse; to denigrate the judges who had rejected their pleas; to strike the pose of injured innocents and work up indignation over the senseless injustice which had been done to them.

Dr Rainy sounded the new rallying-note at a special meeting of Commission held within a few days of the verdict. Referring to the Law Lords, he said, "The idea with which some of these distinguished men seem to be content, the idea of a Church held absolutely and for ever by the faith of men who died 200 or 250 years ago—good men no doubt—that idea is simply to be denounced as thoroughly ungodly. It is an ungodly idea, and the Church or the tribunal that cherishes it is unawares proceeding on fatally wrong principles."[3]

In the vehemence of his polemics the worsted veteran lapsed from his customary caution in his reference to the *Confession* and the men who had produced it. They were "good men no doubt"—and praise could hardly be more faintly expressed; but they had been dead for two centuries or more, and it would be "thoroughly ungodly" to bind men to their theological system. But Dr Rainy's tirade was more rhetorical than logical. "The greatest friend of Truth," says Colton, "is Time." The Supreme

Standard of the Church is the Bible which, because it is the Truth, "endureth to all generations." It was to the formulation and interpretation of this Truth that the Westminster Divines had so loyally devoted their powers. They claimed no infallibility, and invited correction where this might be deemed necessary. But, down the years, the correctness of the *Confession* had not been seriously challenged by the Church. Successive generations of her ministers and other office-bearers had openly and willingly professed their agreement with it—Dr Rainy and his followers included. In the Declaratory Act controversy they had repudiated the charge of divergence from Confessional Standards. Yet now, when the House of Lords had proved the charge against them, they were by implication admitting the truth of it, and devoting all their energy to justifying their change of heart. The Disruption Fathers had unequivocally pledged themselves to the *Confession,* and the Free Church section which had entered the 1900 Union had always claimed to be in that succession. Yet now the "idea" of the judges who ruled that ordination vows, voluntarily taken and never openly called in doubt by those who had taken them, should be honestly observed, was to be denounced as "thoroughly ungodly." It was a strange declaration to be made from a Christian platform.

A leaflet issued around this time by the United Church Advisory Committee is marked by the same strain of disingenuousness. Written by Rev. John Kelman, it affirmed that "No one can join the present Free Church except on two conditions. These are (1) the acceptance of definite and explicit Erastianism . . . (2) the surrender of the right to preach freely to all men the Gospel of the love of God."[4]

According to Kelman's view, the Free Church had acted in Erastian spirit in seeking judgment in an ecclesiastical matter from the Civil Court. Now, that charge would have had substance if the judgment sought had indeed been a purely ecclesiastical or doctrinal one. But the fact was that the Scottish Reformed Church had always recognised the authority of the Civil Court in its own province, and had sought its arbitration in a matter which fell within that province, namely, the ownership of trust funds which were in dispute. It had asked the Civil Courts to examine the Church's Constitution, to declare whether or not the Establishment Principle was part of that Constitution, and whether the Constitution allowed the sweeping powers of change that the United Free Church claimed from it. These were the questions at issue, and they quite properly fell within the province of the civil magistrate. There was no other way in which they could be settled, apart from a complete capitulation on the part of the Free Church to the authoritarianism of the United Free

Church, in which case the Free Church would have become guilty of resiling from the responsibilities of her trusteeship, thereby acquiescing in an unlawful transference of trust funds which had been built up for certain well-defined and clearly defined purposes, to purposes which were patently divergent from the terms of the trust.

An editorial article which appeared in *The Scotsman* at the time (2/8/1904), puts the matter quite bluntly where it says, "The common-sense of the Judges of the highest Court of Appeal in the land had decided that Principal Rainy's Union is a breach of trust. For the Union, it was urged in effect that an institution may depart from the principles and keep the money. To most men this will seem very like dishonesty, and, in effect, it has had the stamp of dishonesty put upon it by the House of Lords. . . . To few men other than those who on the Free Church side carried out the Union would it have occurred to justify breach of trust by spiritual independence. . . . That plea was used. It simply meant that men who act unjustly in a civil court are to escape the legal consequence because they do it with professions of religion in their mouths. Happily the House of Lords has refused to give sanction to such a plea."[4]

The second charge made in the Kelman leaflet referred to, namely, that no one could join the post-1900 Free Church without surrendering "the right to preach freely to all men the Gospel of the love of God," is so pathetically feeble—not to say so blatantly partisan—as to be scarcely worthy of comment. Suffice it to say that the Free Church had not sought modification of, or relief from, her constitutional commitments and doctrinal testimony. Her position was still that of the Disruption Fathers. Like them, she held to the Reformed Faith as formulated in the Westminster Standards. Like them, she was proclaiming the same Gospel as was preached by the great men of Scotland's evangelical succession. If preaching freely to all men "the Gospel of the love of God" was possible only to those who had obscured the Biblical theology of the Scottish Reformers by the liberal universalism of the German schools, then we must revise our estimates of men like Ebenezer and Ralph Erskine, John Love, Andrew Thomson, Thomas Chalmers, Robert Murray McCheyne, Andrew A. Bonar, Alexander Moody Stuart, John MacDonald of Ferintosh and many others of that school. And having done so, we are left with the problem of explaining how the Gospel which they preached was used by God—Whose love (according to Dr Kelman) it failed to reveal—to bring multitudes into His Kingdom and to edify successive generations of the saints.

This reprehensible line of propaganda was widely used by the United Free Church in those years of controversy, and was later brought into the two-volume biography of Principal Rainy by Dr P. Carnegie Simpson—not to the enhancement of his work. Dr Alexander Stewart has dealt faithfully with Carnegie Simpson in *The Free Church of Scotland; 1843-1910,* but perhaps the most scathing criticism of all was the one penned almost half a century later by Dr. Norman Maclean, formerly of St. Cuthbert's Church of Scotland, Edinburgh. "These two ponderous volumes of Dr Simpson's," he writes, "are marked by inaccuracy and the constant imputation of base motives to those who opposed his hero's policy." And he adds, "If only there could be a limit put to the uncritical panegyrics of eloquent biographers! Almost a thousand pages of monotonous eulogy culminated in the judgment that Principal Rainy was 'the greatest living Scotsman.' A. J. Balfour was then at the height of his power; Lord Kelvin was enriching the world; Bell's telephone was revolutionising humanity; other Scottish benefactors were making the world their debtor, but Dr Simpson records Gladstone's estimate of Scotland's greatest man with approval. This is almost the only flash of humour in a thousand pages. Alas! that it should be unconscious!"[5]

Dr Stewart, although keenly critical of Rainy's ecclesiastical policy, pays tribute to the greatness of the man where he writes of him, "He was surrounded by many able men, men with a record of scholarship and solid achievement, but his massive personality overshadowed them all. . . . No one could listen long to his words, even on an ordinary subject, without realising that his was a master mind. There was a breadth of view in his handling of a question, and a note of distinction in his utterance, that marked him out from the common order of men. Neither can there be any doubt as to his courage. The sight of the old man of well-nigh four-score winters staggering to his feet after the tremendous blow of 1st August, 1904, and addressing himself with unconquerable fortitude to the task of restoring the shattered energies of his Church, is one that compels admiration. But in his leadership of the Free Church Dr. Rainy was an undoubted opportunist. . . . In Dr. Masson's luminous phrase he was 'skilled in the science of exigencies'."[6]

Many of his staunchest admirers would agree that, in the balanced phrases of his Free Church critic, Dr Rainy is more worthily commemorated than he is in the oleaginous adulation of his doting Boswell.

The hue and cry raised by the United Free Church was continued through the closing months of 1904 with increasing virulence. When it became necessary from platform or pulpit to refer to the Free Church the adjective was seldom left unqualified. It was the "Wee" Free Church, or the "Legal" Free Church—epithets pregnant with opprobrium, although it is hard to understand why it should be deemed a reproach to be in a minority for conscience sake, or to be judged, by the supreme legislature, to be the legal possessors of a title and property which had been illegally annexed by other claimants!

Sometimes the plots of the agitators backfired against themselves, as in the case of the Hay Thorburn letter.

Mr J. Hay Thorburn, the General Secretary of the Free Church, had written a private letter to a friend, in which he referred to the intimidation and boycotting being practised by the United Free Church against the Free Church, and expressed the hope that the Free Church cause would be supported by the Protestant members of Parliament. But Mr Hay Thorburn had expressed the opinion—in a purely personal capacity—that the United Free Church were "strong supporters of the Irish Home Rule policy," a view for the holding of which he could, no doubt, have given arguable reasons. It happened, however, that his letter was insufficiently addressed, and that in the Post Office's endeavour to return it to the sender, the postman had delivered it at the United Free Church Offices. There it was opened, copied, and then resealed and sent on its way. The copy was given to Rev. Alexander Lee, who had served the pre-1900 Free Church in a secretarial capacity, and was giving similar service to the United Free Church. Mr Lee's "defective scouting" in the Highlands had led to embarrassing misapprehensions on the part of the United Free Church, and now, it seemed to him, he was being given an unforeseen opportunity to regain credit with his masters. So he passed on the copy of Mr Hay Thorburn's letter to Dr Rainy who, that same evening, produced it at a public meeting in Glasgow and disclosed its contents, attaching as much significance to these as if they had been an official pronouncement of the Free Church, but without ever indicating how the letter had come into his possession.

The aggrieved Free Church Secretary immediately, through the public press, demanded an explanation, which, when eventually it was given, brought upon the United Free delinquents the scathing denunciation of the press. Realising too late how his unethical action might damage his own reputation and that of his Church, Dr Rainy published a letter of abject apology, acknowledging "the impropriety of the letter having been copied, and also of its having been used." Similar expressions of regret were forthcoming from other United Free parties involved, and Mr Lee, having again revealed his unhappy capacity for embarrassing his masters, was quietly faded out.

That the commotion which followed the House of Lords decision was part of a deliberate policy devised by the defeated litigants was evident from the high official standing of the men who gave it direction. The idea was to represent the United Free Church as completely frustrated by the obstructive tactics of the successful Free Church appellants who, by their persistent endeavours to gain possession of their churches and manses were wantonly throwing their work into confusion.

The truth of the matter is, however, that the confusion could have been avoided if that had really been the desire and intention of the United Free Church authorities. Meeting on 11th August, 1904, just ten days after the decision of the Lords, the Free Church Commission of Assembly agreed to propose to the United Free Church certain interim arrangements that would give both sides the opportunity to recover from the excitement and upheaval of recent events and take a more sober and objective view of the new situation in which they found themselves. In the main, these proposals were (1) that the Free Church Assembly Hall and Offices be handed over to the Free Church, but with arrangements for the interim accommodation of the United Free Church; (2) that existing Free Church congregations be given possession of their buildings, but, again, with an arrangement for the accommodation of the United Free congregations if these were unable to find suitable accommodation elsewhere; (3) that the United Free Church continue to retain meanwhile all buildings not required by the Free Church; (4) that the Church's Colleges in Glasgow and Aberdeen, and other educational agencies, be left undisturbed for the meanwhile; (5) that the Foreign Missions funds should continue to be applied to United Free Church missions.

These interim arrangements would, according to the Free Church proposal, continue until 30th June of the following year. Originally, there was a stipulation that the buildings being made available to the United Free Church under this temporary arrangement should not be used for attacks on the House of Lords judgment or on the Free Church, or for the disseminating of views contrary to the recognised doctrines and principles on which the trust funds of the Free Church rested, but when the United Free Church objected to the proviso on the ground that it would constitute an undue interference with its liberty it was not insisted upon.

This attempt to call a truce for a few months proved quite abortive. The United Free Church leaders would have none of it, and from the viewpoint of worldly wisdom their policy was undoubtedly right. To accept the Free Church proposals might give the impression that they were ceding to the successful appellants the right of initiative, and they were resolved not to cover themselves with such a humiliation. The recent Union might even yet run into serious trouble unless steps were taken for its immediate consolidation. The law verdict had brought disillusionment to many who had quietly submitted themselves to be herded into the United Free Church, and some were revealing an inclination to retrace their footsteps. There were instances of ministers and congregations returning to their earlier allegiance, and there was a constant danger that this trend might continue. Accordingly, the United Free leaders rejected the suggestions that had been made to them and pressed for an immediate and permanent settlement. The plan was to make it as difficult as possible for the Free Church to regain possession of the buildings which she needed, and to consolidate her position. In many instances interdicts had to be taken out by the Free Church in order to obtain possession of church buildings to which the Lords had established her right. These, of course, had to be granted, whereupon the spokesmen for the United Free congregations raised their voices in loud protest against their opponents, resembling them to the ruthless persecutors who harried the men of the moss-hags in Covenanting times! The purpose of it all was, as J. Boyd Orr shrewdly remarks, "to attract sympathy for themselves and antipathy against their opponents, and force the attention of the Government."

The campaign against the House of Lords and the persistent efforts to bring the law into contempt were all part of this plan. Scornful references were made to the theological dissertations of the jurists in the judgments given, and the Free Church, with its professed zeal for spiritual independence, was charged with the gravest inconsistency because it had called in the civil power to judge in a matter that lay entirely within the province of ecclesiastical and spiritual jurisdiction. But this was a complete distortion of facts. The question submitted to the Law Lords related to the trust funds of the Free Church of Scotland to which two parties were claimants. Allegations had been made by one party that the other had radically changed its constitution, and thereby had forfeited its right to the Church's patrimony. It was necessary for the judges therefore to examine the constitution referred to, and decide whether one or other of the parties had changed its relation to the said constitution, and, if so, whether the change really involved forfeiture of the title and trusts of the Free Church of Scotland. The task assigned them fell properly within their juridical province, and they performed it with the strictest regard to legal rectitude. That another question would subsequently arise—in the event of the judgment going to the Free Church—was obvious from the beginning; and now it had to be faced. Would the legal holders of the trust be able fully to carry it out? Clearly, the Free Church, especially at its numerical strength immediately after the 1900 Union, lacked this ability. In

127

the circumstances, they expected that the part of the trust which they could not administer would be assigned to the larger body who had shared in its administration in the past but was now absorbed in the United Free Church. But how was the ability of the Free Church to be gauged, and by what criterion was the division of the property to be determined?

If the Lords did not provide the answers to these questions it was because they did not lie within their remit. Those answers would have to come from Parliament, as eventually they did.

A competent and important assessment of the House of Lords judgment was contributed to *The Times* by a former Lord Justice of the Court of Appeal, Sir Edward Fry. In a refutation of the reckless charges made by certain United Free spokesmen to the effect that the judgment "rested upon a forced application of the doctrine of trusts." a doctrine which, as he says, "lies at the root of almost all our domestic and social and philanthropic life," he asks, "What would come to our family arrangements, to our benevolent institutions, to the chapels and other property of our non-conformist bodies, if the doctrine of the sacredness of trusts were shaken by a decision of the House of Lords, and if it should be held that a majority of those interested could divert from its original purpose property contributed by those who had declared the objects of their bounty?" Ridiculing the view that English judges were incapable of appreciating the subtleties of Scottish Presbyterianism and its theology, he points out that of the seven Lords who heard the appeal, one was a Scotsman; two were Irishmen; and four were English! And he adds, "to assert that Presbyterianism is something so special, so transcendental, so marvellous, as to be unintelligible to any Englishman, however trained to apprehend and weigh facts, is to my Southern intellect a highly doubtful proposition." Referring to the argument that the judgment precluded "all advance, all progress in doctrine, all evolution, to use the modern phrase, in any religious body," he retorts, "It does nothing of the sort. It only lays down that if a body by any process of evolution departs from the doctrine for the promulgation of which it has accepted property, it may not carry that property with it, or divert it to new ends."[7]

Sir Edward allows that "any church, or other body, may, if it thinks fit, stipulate in its original constitution for the liberty to change its doctrine or its practice, and then any property given to support that constitution will be as much available for the new as for the old objects of the body. You may change as much as you like," he adds, "but you must not apply to one purpose money given you for another."

That was the crux of the whole matter. There was no "forced
128

application of the doctrine of trusts"; it was the only application that legal principle and precedent could justify.

Another lawyer, writing in the *Edinburgh Evening Dispatch,* of 24th April, 1905, and disclaiming connection with the Free Church of Scotland, bears supporting testimony. The Free Church, he says, had never claimed that they could administer the whole property. "Their position from the first has been that they were only in a position to administer part of the trust.

"It appears to me therefore, that the present position, attitude and procedure of the Free Church are perfectly defensible. They are bound by the judgment of the House of Lords to take possession of the property, churches and manses, the Trusts in connection with which they can show they are in a position to fulfil. No hostile criticism of their actings, nor sneers at the smallness of their numbers or the insignificance of their personalities should deter them from doing their bounden duty, and one cannot but admire the pluck and fearlessness of the men, who in spite of what is happening, go calmly forward in an endeavour to perform the functions which the House of Lords declared it was theirs alone to fulfil.

"My plea is that the Free Church has been maligned and their position distorted. It was not only their right, but their duty, to implement the House of Lords' judgment, and if their progress has been slow in asserting their rights, the cause is to be found in the obstructive tactics of a party who had forfeited all right, title or interest in the church property."

During this period of harassment and misrepresentation however, the Free Church had her consolations and encouragements apart altogether from the justification which had come to her from the House of Lords judgment. Her ecclesiastical neighbours, the Reformed Presbyterian Church and the United Original Secession Church, had been helpful in a variety of ways. Several Church of Scotland ministers kindly offered the comfort of their buildings to homeless congregations, and among the United Free ministers and people there were not a few who dissociated themselves from the unkindly treatment that was being meted out to the Free Church by the denomination to which they belonged.

1. G. Reith, *Reminiscences of the United Free Church General Assembly;* p. 53.
2. Stewart and Cameron, *Free Church of Scotland 1843-1910;* p. 248.
3. ibid. p. 269.
4. *The Scotsman,* 2nd August 1904.
5. Norman Maclean, *Set Free;* pp. 130, 132.
6. Stewart and Cameron, *Free Church of Scotland 1843-1910;* pp. 54, 55.
7. Kennedy Cameron, *Scottish Church Union 1900;* pp. 98, 99.

CHAPTER SEVENTEEN

ENCOURAGEMENT AND DISAPPOINTMENT

Venture to take the wind on your face for Christ.—*Samuel Rutherford.*

It was a reasonable expectation that the Free Presbyterian Church which had gone out in 1893 should show sympathy with men who had been their former brethren in the Constitutional party, and express gratification at their victory; and this some of them did. At a Synod held in November 1904, the Rev. John R. Mackay moved a resolution which said: "The Synod cannot pass unnoticed the decision of the House of Lords of 1st August 1904 in the great Scottish Church case. The Synod would express its sincere satisfaction with that decision insomuch as by it the highest Court of Appeal in this land has sustained the view which has always been held in this Church, that the Establishment Principle was essential to the original Free Church Constitution. The Synod would also express its satisfaction that by this decision the Barrier Act of 1697 has been so interpreted as to do away with the semblance of reason which the respondents in this case sought to give for that extravagant and despotic claim of Church power advocated by them. . . ."[1]

The motion for the adoption of this resolution was seconded by the Rev. Alexander Macrae, but some members felt that it did not go far enough. Accordingly, the Rev. George Mackay tabled the following dissent: "We, the undersigned, on behalf of ourselves and as many as agree with us, while satisfied with the resolution of Synod, so far as it goes, feel called upon to record our dissatisfaction (1) that it does not sufficiently recognise that the judgment of the House of Lords in the Church case, and the circumstances attending the same, may justly be regarded as a remarkable indication of the divine displeasure against the majority of the Free Church who entered the Union of 1900, for their grievous betrayal of truth, and (2) that it makes no direct reference to the present Free Church as the instrument, under divine providence, through which the decision has been obtained, and contains no adequate expression of kindly feeling towards it in its present difficult position."[2]

Mr Mackay's co-signatories in this dissent were Rev. Alexander Stewart, Rev. James P. Sinclair, Mr W. R. T. Sinclair and Mr John MacNeilage. All of these later returned to the Free Church— Mr (later Dr) Stewart, who was followed by the majority of his congregation, to continue his ministry in what became Fountainbridge Free Church, Edinburgh, until it was later amalgamated with St Columba Free Church, with Mr Stewart as minister. The Rev. J. P. Sinclair became minister of Olrig Free Church, and the Rev. George Mackay became pastor of Stornoway Free Church, and afterwards of Fearn Free Church. Mr John MacNeilage later became minister of Bower Free Church, and Mr W. R. T. Sinclair, a successful business man in Edinburgh, gave notable service to the Free Church in a variety of ways, and was for many years one of its General Trustees.

It is interesting to note that the movers of the resolution against which these brethren had dissented on the grounds of its inadequacy, after an interval of fourteen years, rejoined their former brethren in the ministry of the Free Church, Mr Mackay to become Professor of New Testament in the Free Church College, and a Doctor of Divinity of St Andrews University, and Mr Macrae to become minister of Maryburgh Free Church.

Of the ministers who returned to the Free Church from the Free Presbyterian Church, after the 1900 Union, the first to show his sympathy with the Free Church remnant who had continued loyal to the Church's historic testimony was the Rev. John Macleod. No sooner did the remanent Free Church repeal the Declaratory Act of 1892 than Mr Macleod came to the aid of the Training of the Ministry Committee of the Free Church by serving as lecturer in the departments of New Testament and Systematic Theology in the Free Church College.

Mr Macleod, a brilliant scholar, thoroughly devoted to the Reformed Faith, took the view that, with the Declaratory Act of 1892 which had caused the Free Presbyterian secession now expunged from the statute-book of the Free Church, there should be immediate conference between these two bodies with a view to re-union. Accordingly, at a meeting of Synod in November 1905, he moved for the appointment of a committee to meet with a committee of the Free Church for the discussion of the question. His motion was defeated by an amendment moved by Rev. Neil Cameron, whereupon Mr Macleod tabled his dissent "inasmuch as by refusing even to hold a conference, a policy of division and disunion is being pursued, and what does not justify the making of a separation does not justify the maintaining of it."[3]

This dissent was signed by Rev. Alexander Stewart and Rev. George Mackay as well as Rev. John Macleod, who declared their intention to do whatever they could "to heal the breach between the two branches of the Free Church adhering to its Disruption position."[4] After consultation with the Free Church, they were cordially admitted to its ministry in December of that same year—Mr Macleod to become Professor of New Testament in the

Free Church College. In 1913 he accepted a call to the pastorate of the Free North Church, Inverness, but was recalled to the teaching staff of the College as Professor of Apologetics and Pastoral Theology in 1930. In 1927 he had been given the Doctorate of Divinity by the University of Aberdeen, and had become Principal of the Free Church College while still in his Inverness pastorate.

Less than five years after his admission to the Free Church, Dr Alexander Stewart took the leading part in writing the vindication of the Free Church which appeared under the title of *The Free Church of Scotland, 1843-1910;* and in 1917 he succeeded Mr Archibald MacNeilage as editor of *The Free Church Monthly Record.*

Several other ministers from the Free Presbyterian Church joined the Free Church in the years that followed and made their valuable contribution to the expanding work of the Church at home and abroad.

The agitation raised by the United Free Church after the House of Lords decision in favour of the Free Church yielded the result for which they had laboured. Parliamentary action was taken.

The Free Church had already signified its readiness, once the measure of its capacity to administer the Trust had been ascertained, to welcome the lawful authority which should undertake to administer the Trust which might be reckoned beyond the capacity of the Free Church to use and administer. The authority to adjudicate in the dividing of the Trust, they insisted, was to be found "only in the Sovereign Power of the realm." They would not themselves transfer any part of the Trust funds or property to the United Free Church inasmuch as this would mean their connivance at an arrangement whereby funds that had been "destined to a Church bound to maintain the Bible as the Word of God and the whole doctrine of the Confession of Faith," and to adhere to the Establishment Principle, to purposes entirely different, viz., "the endowment of Voluntaryism," and "the promotion of latitudinarian views."[4] They were ready to accept the responsibility of applying the Trust to the purposes for which it had been created, to the utmost of their capacity, and their request for a delay in coming to a final decision until June of the following year was in order to ascertain with greater accuracy than was as yet possible what the limits of that capacity were. If the Trust, or any part of it, was to be alienated from its original purpose and applied to another, the responsibility for the action would then lie with the State.

But sensing that precipitate action would be to their own advantage, and to the serious inconvenience of the Free Church, the United Free leaders, using their very considerable political influence, kept up their pressure on the Government and secured the appointment of a Royal Commission to take the matter in hand immediately.

Actually, two Commissions were appointed, a Royal Commission "to inquire into all the facts connected with the said funds, and to report as to whether any or what action should be taken thereon by legislation or otherwise," and a Departmental Commission, for the purpose of making temporary arrangements for the use of congregational property by the opposing parties, pending a permanent settlement.

The Departmental Commission, under Sir John Cheyne, made heavy weather from the outset, and it became evident that, in the circumstances of that period of turmoil, joint-occupancy of the buildings in dispute was not a practicable solution. Neither side was satisfied—although for different reasons—with the procedural plans outlined by Sir John; and eventually, the Free Church withdrew from the Commission altogether.

The Royal Commission fared more happily. Lord Balfour of Burleigh was first proposed as its chairman, but memories of his part in the gunboat expedition to Lewis were still fresh, and he was passed over in favour of Lord Elgin, whose fellow-Commissioners were Lord Kinnear and Sir Ralph Anstruther. The Free Church, by its Commission of Assembly, had already indicated its readiness—once the limits of its capacity had been fairly ascertained—not only to "loyally submit to, but gladly welcome," the Royal Commission as "the lawful authority which should undertake to administer the remainder" of the Trust. The authority which should carry out this work, they said, was to be found "only in the Sovereign Power of the realm," They declined, on their own responsibility, to transfer any part of the trust-funds and property of the pre-1900 Free Church to the United Free Church because it would mean the endowment of Voluntaryism, and the application "for the promotion of latitudinarian views" of funds which had been "destined to a Church bound to maintain the Bible as the Word of God, and the whole doctrine of the Confession of Faith."[5] In the event of such a transference being effected, the responsibility for the alienation of the Trust from its original purpose would lie with the State and not with the Free Church.

In the inquiry under Lord Elgin the United Free Church had an obvious advantage. The documents relating to the Trust were in their hands and, led by men of quite outstanding ability, they had done their home-work thoroughly and were ready with their arguments. In presenting their claims they urged that the intentions of the donors to the Trust funds of the Free Church should be taken into serious consideration by the Commission. But this the Commission declined to do, and with good reason. The aims and objects of the Free Church had been clearly defined and publicly proclaimed from the beginning, and the actions of the good people who had built up her Trust funds by their gifts and legacies could only be understood as signifying their agreement and sympathy with her declared purposes. How to check up with them now and ascertain their precise intentions was something which, to say the least, lay beyond the normal activities of a Parliamentary Commission! To obtain more explicit evidence of intention from living donors was another matter, and due weight might be given to it; but if they came forward now to submit reasons why their gifts should not be included in funds that were to go to the maintenance of Free Church testimony was evidence that they had changed their mind regarding that testimony, or, perhaps, that they had not properly understood it from the beginning. For the principles and creed of the Free Church of Scotland remained what they had always been.

The Royal Commission submitted its report on 19th April, 1905. Finding that the Free Church, in its reduced strength, was "unable adequately to execute the Trusts of all the endowments," they recommended the appointment by Parliament of an Executive Commission to divide the funds and properties of the Free Church of Scotland between the rival claimants. They urged that, in this allocation, "liberal provision" should be made "for the equipment of the Free Church for its mission as a Christian Church according to the standard which prevails in other Presbyterian Churches in Scotland." The Free Church was the legal heir to these properties. The allocation to the United Free Church of an interest in them was solely in respect of the fact that she was the next of kin to the Free Church and had already enjoyed benefit from the Trust.

Referring to the unhappy relations now existing between the two Churches concerned in their investigation, the Commission, with appropriate impartiality, found that faults existed on both sides, although not in equal proportions. The following paragraph in their Report makes this quite clear. For, after regretting a disposition, on the part of the Free Church, to press too hastily and too insistently for the recognition of their legal rights, they say: "It is not part of our duty to investigate the causes which have developed into the extreme bitterness now existing, but we think it right to say that we much regret that, during the stage of the controversy between the separation in 1900 and the legal determination of the proprietary rights in 1904, the minority did not receive more consideration at the hands of the majority. A more generous policy then would have been a wiser and more far-seeing policy, and would scarcely have failed to bear fruit now."[6]

The Commission advised that the property covered by the Trust should be vested in the proposed Executive Commission, but the recommendation was not given effect to by Parliament. Thus the supremacy of law was acknowledged, and the decision of the House of Lords was honoured.

1. *History of the Free Presbyterian Church of Scotland;* p. 138.
2. ibid. p. 139.
3. ibid. p. 146.
4. Stewart and Cameron, *Free Church of Scotland 1843-1910;* p. 297.
5. ibid. p. 298.

CHAPTER EIGHTEEN

THE SETTLEMENT BY PARLIAMENT

It is a comfort to all that lay the interests of God's Israel near their hearts that Israel's God is the same that made the world, and can secure the Church in times of the greatest danger and distress.—Matthew Henry.

While the Government Bill regarding the appointment of the Executive Commission was being prepared, the General Assemblies met in Edinburgh and prepared for the final phase of the dispute. The United Free Church, in anticipation of receiving the larger share of the Trust funds and property, drew up a set of Resolutions for submission to Parliament, setting forth the terms on which she proposed to hold the allocation that might be made to her. She affirmed her power to alter her subordinate standards and formulas, and asserted that her procedure for the future should be that "in all the courts of the Church, the decision of the Court given either unanimously, or by a majority of its members present and voting thereat, is the decision of the Court, and the decision of the General Assembly so reached is final."

All the funds and properties of the United Free Church, both present and future, were now to be held in conformity with these principles, it being, however, "open to the Church to accept any benefaction subject to any specific conditions which the donor may attach thereto."

The redoubtable Dr Rainy was again in the forefront to build up the fullest possible political advantage for his Church. An election was in the offing, and as the man with the big battalions under his command, he could barter his offer of influence at the polls for promises of support in the House of Commons. Letters were sent to all ministers of the United Free Church urging them to use their local influence politically. "It is hoped," wrote Dr Rainy, "that you will, with the help, when possible, of one or two intelligent and influential friends, apply to voters of weight in your constituency asking them to write as soon as possible to their M.P.s, expressing the strong desire that the Bill should be amended and brought into conformity with the recommendations of the Royal Commission. Letters from voters who agree with them politically are especially important. In all that is done, members of our Church on both sides of politics should act together."[1] Nothing mattered for the moment but that the utmost

Parliamentary power should be built up to offset the much-execrated House of Lords decision in favour of the Free Church.

The Free Church, on her part, resolved that the best representation she could make to Parliament at this juncture would be to submit again her Claim of Rights as had been done before by the Disruption Fathers over sixty years previously. The minority who had decided to continue the Free Church in 1900 had claimed to be in true descent from those honoured leaders when the bond linking them to the State had to be broken in the interests of spiritual independence. And their claim had been upheld by the highest legislature in the land. They needed no stronger argument in the Parliamentary action that was now proceeding than to resubmit the historic document by which the Free Church had been identified on that former occasion.

Under her revised Constitution the United Free Church now awarded herself the power to chop and change her avowed principles, to divert her property and funds from the purposes to which they had been expressly designated, and, even by the slimmest majority in the General Assembly, to disinherit any minority of men who might feel themselves unable to resile from solemn pledges, which they had given at their ordination to office, now to take up a position utterly inconsistent therewith. All this was an obvious backwash from the recent House of Lords decision. The innovators had learned their lesson. No longer should the Church be bound so closely to any Constitution or formula as to jeopardise the daring innovators. No longer would there be any serious risk of trials for heresy. No longer would it be possible for a minority to overturn the well-laid plans of the party in power, as had so recently been done. Might would be right! The new resolutions adopted by the United Free Church meant, as Dr Alexander Stewart puts it, "the practical annihilation of the rights of minorities."[2]

The Churches (Scotland) Act was introduced in the House of Commons in June 1905. Under its provisions the Free Church was to be held entitled to congregational property in every instance in which they were able to show that "out of those who in the opinion of the Commission were members or adherents of the congregation on the 30th day of October 1900, and are, at the commencement of this Act both resident in the district, and members or adherents of the Free Church or United Free Church congregation, at least one-third are members or adherents of the Free Church congregation. . . ."[3]

Furthermore, the Commission were instructed, in making their allocation under the Act, to have regard "to congregational contributions and other income of the Free Church," and "make adequate provision for the education of the students for the

J

ministry of the Free Church, for the support, subject to payment of the usual annual contributions (if any) of aged and infirm ministers and of widows and orphans of ministers of that Church, for the support of ministers of Free Church congregations to which congregational property has been allocated under this Act, for itinerant preachers, and for the general purposes of administration and management of that Church. . . ."[4]

The proportion of one-third might have appeared reasonable and fair had the numerical strength of the congregations been reckoned as at a date subsequent to the House of Lords judgment, but pressure was exerted on Parliament to stipulate that the reckoning of comparative congregational strength be made as at 30th October, 1900, a date when, in the existing confusion, the strength of the remanant Free Church congregations could not be assessed with any degree of accuracy. Many sympathisers were still uncertain as to what they ought to do. Some, whose hearts were with the struggling minority, were still hesitating to cast in their lot with them partly from uncertainty as to their prospects of survival, and partly, in many cases, from an understandable reluctance to leave the old church buildings in which their forebears had worshipped and which had become very dear to them from hallowed associations. A rushed reckoning would obviously be to the advantage of the United Free Church, for a one-third assessment of the Free Church congregations in 1900 would be much less, in many districts, than a similar proportion of the same congregations in 1905.

The Executive Commission appointed to carry through the allocation of property consisted of the three members of the Royal Commission with the addition of Sir Thomas Gibson Carmichael and Sir Charles B. Logan. Sir Charles died in March 1907, and soon thereafter Sir Thomas was appointed Governor of Victoria. Sheriff Crawford was added to the Commission in 1908, and with his appointment another strong partisan of the United Free Church appeared in the seats of power. Lord Elgin, as chairman of the Commission, won the praise of both parties by his fairness and courtesy, and by his painstaking efforts to maintain a complete impartiality throughout all the proceedings.

His work was far from easy. In estimating the stipulated one-third of the numerical strength of a congregation, in members and adherents, an understanding had to be reached as to what constituted an "adherent." The definition agreed upon was taken from an Act of Assembly of 1874 which, in addition to non-communicant seat-holders, included under the term adherent, "all persons above fourteen years of age who, by their attendance at a particular church, make it to be understood that it is their

138

habitual place of worship, and that they are connected with or adhered to the congregation."[5]

But such rolls of adherents in congregations, where they existed were, as indeed they still are, notoriously unreliable, and it is not surprising that the Commission had difficulty in assessing some of them. There were cases where the rolls had not been revised for years, with the result that many, whose names were still on them, had left the districts, whereas others had come into the districts and had been resident there for some years, whose names had not been added. Inevitably, there were cases where the statistics supplied to the Commission by both sides in the dispute were challenged, and had to be investigated by neutral Assistant-Commssioners who were authorised to deal with local disputes. Surprised at the numbers who were claiming connection with the Free Church, spokesmen of the United Free Church alleged that the Free Church were claiming as adherents men and women who, at the date of Union, were non-churchgoers. Such allegations were carefully investigated, and proved to be to the discredit of those who made them. One of the Assistant Commissioners, Mr James Adam, towards the end of the local enquiries, asked Mr Burnett-Stewart, Agent for the United Free Church, whether he had found any trace of the "stage army" which the Free Church were charged with having used. Mr Burnett-Stewart admitted that he had not. "Neither have I," replied Mr Adam.[6]

Even after the Commission had completed their division of the property some of the United Free leaders continued their campaign against the Free Church. Dr Robert Howie, for example, alleged that upwards of fifty of the manses allocated to the Free Church were not being used in any way except, indeed, that they provided lodging for tramps and rats! The statement was immediately taken up by Mr Archibald MacNeilage, Editor of *The Free Church Monthly Record*, who challenged Dr Howie to name the manses that were not being "utilised in any way" by the Free Church. Dr Howie replied that what he had meant was that the manses he had in mind were not being utilised "as manses for settled ministers" — a somewhat modified version of the original statement! It ought to have been obvious to all except the most purblind critic that, in the prevailing circumstances, some of those houses were not likely to have permanent ministerial occupants for some time to come and would be used temporarily to house the resident lay-preachers who were sent to supply the vacant congregations during rather prolonged vacancies. But the stories of ruinous dilapidation were proved to be wild exaggerations. A representative of *The Scotsman* was sent to investigate the situation, at the instigation, it was believed, of a prominent shipping magnate, who desired to use the information that might thus be obtained as the ground for another approach to Parliament in the interests of the United Free Church. The research was abortive; for *The Scotsman*, in due course, reported that "the sensational statements depicting these deserted Highland homes as given over to rats and tramps" were discredited. "Our correspondent," so runs the newspaper report, "has demonstrated that there is no warrant for the suggestion that Church property is falling to ruin, and that the scandal in this dilapidation is so great as to call for the intervention of Parliament. . . . Two dozen so-called derelict manses have been visited, and only three have suffered seriously since they were assigned to the Free Church." And in these three cases, remarks Dr J. Kennedy Cameron, the dilapidation "was in large measure due to windows being maliciously broken by persons unknown, presumably by persons unfriendly to the Free Church."[6]

Altogether it was a sad period in Scottish Church relations. In the interests of "unity" the majority party in the Free Church of Scotland had wrecked their own denomination, sending the Free Presbyterians into secession in 1893, and doing their utmost to crush out of existence the Constitutionalist minority who had banded themselves together to maintain and defend the evangelical and Reformed testimony of the Disruption Fathers, a testimony which had been hallowed by martyr blood in days of persecution. In many parts of the country, and over the Highland area in particular, instead of reducing the number of Presbyterian denominations, they added two — the Free Presbyterian Church and the United Free Church. Ironically, over vast areas of the country where scarcely a single member of the United Presbyterian communion could be found, they split the existing Free Church for the sake of union with a denomination that was utterly without representation in the area. With Free Church funds, to which the House of Lords had declared they had no right or title, they built United Free places of worship, many of which are today serving the more mundane purposes of village halls and community centres — even of furniture stores and sale rooms.

The charges of persecution brought against the Free Church by their opponents in those days have long since been revealed in their complete absurdity. "It was declared," writes J. Boyd Orr, "that they (the United Free Church), were undergoing the experiences of the Covenanters, and people were left to picture the modern 'killing times', with the Lord Chancellor as the 'bloody Clavers' and the 'Wee Frees' as his dragoons. The only difficulty was to fill in the item of suffering. All this was the sheerest cant. The U.F. Church was rich and influential. In every case it had ample accommodation, with the minimum of inconvenience. In Edinburgh the Free Church claimed one church out of 40 which she legally possessed; in Kirkcaldy, 1 out of 9; in Dundee, 1 out of 33; and so on . . . and no U.F. minister has been ejected from a manse."[8]

Possession of the Free Church's headquarter buildings on the Mound, in Edinburgh, was strongly claimed by both parties. The reason for this was not far to seek, and, indeed, it was clearly stated by Professor Kennedy Cameron in the conclusion of his evidence before the Commission. "The Mound buildings," he said, "are, so to speak, the citadel. The College, Assembly Hall and Offices are so closely and vitally connected with the history of the Free Church that to alienate them now would be, in my opinion, to strike a blow at the most visible symbol of the Church as the historical Free Church."

The argument bore weight with the Royal Commission and influenced the ultimate settlement.

Although the Free Church claimants were well aware that the New College and Assembly Hall buildings were inconveniently large for their purposes at the time, and for the foreseeable future, they also knew that they must bid boldly if they were to have any hope of staying on the Mound. Relinquishing the Free Church Colleges of Glasgow and Aberdeen to the United Free Church, they claimed the New College, Edinburgh, and for one year actually occupied it. They were willing that the United Free Church should have the Assembly Hall, but, in exchange, they claimed the Free High Church (now New College Library) as an Assembly Hall for the Free Church. This proposed division of the Mound property was understandably regarded by the Executive Commission as an awkward one, since it would have meant that the two Assembly Halls would have been situated on the same quadrangle. Eventually, the Free Church Offices block, with its beautiful Presbytery Hall, was assigned to the Free Church for College and Offices accommodation; and St John's Free Church, across the Lawnmarket from the old Free Church Assembly Hall (now the Assembly Hall of the Church of Scotland), was allocated to the Free Church to serve both as an Assembly Hall and a place of worship for the disinherited Free St Columba's congregation. The St John's United Free congregation were joined with the Martyrs' congregation on George IV Bridge. On leaving their old church they took with them the massive stone plaque of Dr Guthrie, the famous first minister of St John's, and installed it in their new quarters, where, for over sixty years, its inscription misleadingly proclaimed to the visitor that Guthrie was "the first minister of this Church." But with the disbanding of the Martyrs' and St

John's congregation in 1973, Guthrie's plaque was restored to its former setting in Free St John's, now Free St Columba's.

In towns where the Free Church could not make the stipulated one-third in any of the congregations, and where there were minority groups ready to be consolidated as one congregation of the Free Church of Scotland, such congregations were provided for under the "special arrangements" and "exceptional treatment" clauses of the Executive Commission's remit.

The Executive Commission finished its work of apportionment in 1909, and the final lines of division were drawn. On the whole it had carried out its difficult task with a commendable consideration for fairness and equity. But underlying its decisions was the assumption that long life and wide expansion were not to be looked for in the attenuated Free Church of Scotland. She had grown considerably, it was true, in the nine years since 1900, but the growth, according to her United Free opponents, had been forced and unreal. She must therefore be deemed to have reached maturity, and her measure must be taken accordingly. Her capacity for administering the pre-Union trust of the Free Church of Scotland must be assumed to be indicated by her numerical and congregational strength towards the end of the year 1900. This arrangement was, and increasingly became, a grievous disadvantage to the Free Church as her work continued to expand at home and abroad. But her leaders and their loyal supporters had achieved their principal purpose. They had secured the continuance in Scotland of the Reformed Faith as formulated in the *Westminster Confession*. They had maintained the God-honoured testimony of the Evangelical Party in the Church of Scotland who had founded the Free Church of Scotland in 1843. They had kept faith with the God-fearing benefactors of the Free Church by ensuring that as much as had been allocated to them of the Church's property and trust should be retained for the purposes to which the donors had designated them. They had redeemed the law of trusteeship from the reproach to which it had been subjected. And, not least important, they had borne a nation-wide testimony to the basic doctrines of the Christian Gospel in a time of doctrinal confusion and theological disorder when men were teaching that it was possible — as Carlyle put it — to "hold the premises of German unbelief and draw the conclusions of Scottish Evangelical orthodoxy."[9]

Three-quarters of a century have passed since the Free Church minority made their historic stand, and many who were critical of them then lived to see, and were honest enough to acknowledge, that what they did in that hour of crisis was for the Christian good of Scotland.

The ending of the Executive Commission's adjudication meant that the Free Church was now able to devote fuller attention to her recovery at home and abroad. In the home field her ministers had been labouring under extreme pressure, for their numbers were few, and the pastorless charges under their care many. Now, with a fully staffed College, she was training her own students, and her ministry rapidly increased. But while problems in the home field were being solved the situation in the mission fields of the Church presented a daunting challenge, for all the missionaries — many of them not realising at the time the true issues of the Church situation at home — had entered the United Free Church, taking with them the native congregations, most of whom were quite unaware of the doctrinal shift in the home Church.

The Free Church's resources in manpower and finance at the time were so strained that the prospect of her being able to fulfil the purposes of the trust with respect to foreign missions seemed faint indeed. It was this situation, no doubt, that decided the Executive Commission to allocate her a mere £25,000 for her work in the mission field. This sum yielded only an annual income of about £1,000 at the existing rate of interest. It was therefore no small indication of the Church's zeal for bringing the Gospel to the heathen and the under-privileged that, in the straitened financial circumstances in which she was left she planned for work in three continents as well as for the maintenance of mission work among the Jews. That zeal for missionary work abroad, carried over from former years, is as marked in the Free Church of today as it ever was in her stronger past.

The Free Church had informed the Executive Commission that they "did not desire to intrude upon any sphere formerly occupied by the Free Church and now taken over by the United Free Church." They made it clear, however, that they proposed to work "in some part of the African continent" because of the Free Church's long association with that field. Accordingly, in 1905, Principal J. D. MacCulloch was sent to South Africa to survey the field and to bring recommendations to the General Assembly as to where the Free Church should resume missionary work there. His work was facilitated by the course of events, and when he returned he brought with him a petition containing more than 4,000 signatures from the native Churches desiring that their connection with the Free Church of Scotland be renewed. They had been assured that the Church Union which had been effected in Scotland had been brought about without any departure from the witness of the Free Church of Scotland, and that the Free Church had been completely merged in the United Free Church. When more accurate information had percolated through from

Scotland they realised that they had been misled, and they requested their mother Church to resume work among them.

Considerable correspondence followed, and in 1907 Principal MacCulloch, accompanied by Professor John Macleod, visited the field again, and, with authority from the General Assembly, resuscitated the former Presbytery of Kaffraria and ordained two native pastors. In the following year the Rev. Alexander Dewar, a native of Lochgilphead, was appointed as the first post-1900 missionary from the homeland to the South African mission. Other missionaries followed, and gradually the work of the mission was built up.

In India also the work of the Free Church mission had to make a new beginning. The United Original Secession Church had a well-equipped mission at Seoni in the Central Provinces, and it was to this mission that the first post-1900 Free Church missionary to India was sent when, in 1905, Miss Elizabeth Macleod, a daughter of Rev. Ewan Macleod, one of the ministers who continued the Free Church in 1900, took up duties as a Bible-woman there. She was joined in 1921 by Dr Annie M. Mackay, a daughter of the Rev. Angus Mackay of Kingussie Free Church. In 1925 Dr Mackay began medical work in Chhapara as a missionary of the Free Church, and two years later, after the Rev. Evan Mackenzie, formerly of the Church of Scotland mission in Kalimpong, had been admitted to the Free Church, a wide area formerly included in the United Original Secession Mission, was taken over by the Free Church as its mission field in India. The two missions worked side by side in the fullest Christian co-operation, and the work, though faith-testing in its extraordinary difficulties, continues to make progress.

A further extension of Free Church missionary activity was made in 1916 when the Free Church mission in Peru was initiated. Beginning in Lima as an educational mission (although the evangelistic side of the work was not overlooked), it quickly acquired a widespread influence under the guidance of Dr John A. Mackay, later President of Princeton Theological Seminary. Other pioneers in the Peruvian Mission were the Rev. J. Calvin Mackay and Sister Sarah Macdougall, who, with their helpers, braved sustained persecution and opposition before they eventually won the support of the local authorities and were enabled to lay firm foundations for the mission in Cajamarca. A medical mission at Moyobamba, originally founded by two well-known pioneer missionary nurses, Miss Soper and Miss Gould, was taken over by the Free Church under the supervision of Dr Kenneth A. Mackay. Dr Mackay's work was shared by a succession of devoted missionary nurses from Scotland, and much useful service was rendered to a very needy community.

It would have been out of character for the Free Church of Scotland to forget her obligation to the Jews. In this connection, however, she used the International Society for the Evangelisation of the Jews as her missionary arm, and the partnership has been cordial and fruitful over the years.

Conditions in Scotland, and particularly in the Highland area, led to widespread emigration to Canada and the United States of America, and the Free Church followed her exiled people to their new homes and helped them to settle there by providing them with Gospel services such as they were used to in the homeland. After the 1929 Church Union in Scotland a group of congregations in Prince Edward Island which had long been loosely connected with the Church of Scotland sought, and were given, affiliation with the Free Church, and their accession became a strengthening of the Free Church cause in Canada.

In Australia the Free Presbyterian Church of Eastern Australia had been in close fellowship with the Free Church of Scotland for many years and, in 1952, legislation was passed whereby mutual eligibility was established between these two bodies. In such ways, the Free Church endeavours to co-operate with like-minded Churches in other lands, and thus to keep faith with the Disruption Fathers into whose labours she entered.

1. Stewart and Cameron, *Free Church of Scotland 1843-1910;* p. 307.
2. ibid. p. 319.
3. Kennedy Cameron, *Scottish Church Union of 1900;* p. 133.
4. ibid. p. 136.
5. Boyd Orr, *Scotch Church Crisis;* p. 79.
6. ibid. p. 90.

CHAPTER NINETEEN

THE MOVE TOWARD WIDER UNION

In many communities the Church has become a social club, and her weekly programmes have not been related to the vital message of the Church. The Church has lost the saltiness of vital doctrines and holy living. Merely including all Churches under one organisation would not vitalise her life and make an impression on the world.—*J. Marcellus Kik.*

The situation in which the United Free Church found herself after the House of Lords decision of 1904 was seized upon by the Church of Scotland to her own advantage. The new theology of the critical schools had entered deeply into her teaching, and many were envious of the liberation from strict confessional obligations which the Free Church had secured for herself by her declaratory legislation, and would fain work out a similar deliverance for themselves. But such action by an Established Church would require Parliamentary sanction, and the times did not favour such a move. A widespread and influential campaign for the disestablishment of the Church of Scotland had been proceeding for several years, and, indeed, had become one of the planks of the Liberal party in their political campaign. For the Established Church, in these circumstances, to ask Parliament for permission to change her time-honoured formula might well prove disastrous; so the counsel of prudence prevailed.*

In the post-1900 troubles of the United Free Church, however, the Church of Scotland saw her opportunity. She could muster considerable political influence which could well prove decisive when the Act for the settling of questions between the Free Church and the United Free Church of Scotland came before Parliament. If, therefore, they made a pact with the United Free Church, guaranteeing support for the Act provided that it contained the clause "and to make amendments of the law with respect to the Church of Scotland" both parties would stand to gain. The Act would be sure of a smooth passage, and the Church of Scotland

---

* In an address given in Glasgow in 1892, the Rev. C. A. Bannatyne said: "So tightly is the Church of Scotland tied to the *Confession* that I have often heard a pre-Disruption minister relate, with much gusto, a tradition how Principal Robertson, thereby, on one occasion, gave their quietus to a jubilant band of extreme Moderates who wished to lead a crusade against that venerable standard. The Principal knew his men and replied, 'O yes, we have a great majority, and could easily do away with the *Confession*,' but ended *sotto voce*, 'only we would a' lose oor livings'."

The zeal of the crusaders wilted at the thought!

would secure the right to treat her formula as the United Free Church was already treating hers. In her straits the United Free Church leaders accepted the proposal, and the Act was given an easy passage. Dr George Reith, in a reference to this agreement, writes: "The inclusion of the famous Clause 5 in the Act raised some feeling in not a few United Free Churchmen, which, however, did not find expression beyond an occasional *obiter dictum,* sarcastic or ironical, aimed at the clever use the Church of Scotland had made of her neighbour's difficulties to secure benefits for herself. The clause granted a long-desired relaxation of the stringent ties that bound the ministry of that Church to the Westminster Confession of Faith."[1]

In an article which he contributed to the *Princeton Theological Review* (April 1926), Dr John Macleod referred to this action by the Church of Scotland as "one of the meanest things in the history of their Church or country". In the highest assessment, it could hardly be cited as an example of scrupulous churchmanship, yet it marked the beginnings of the wider ecclesiastical union which brought these two denominations together in 1929.

The Church of Scotland soon used the liberty thus secured when, in 1909, she changed the formula binding her office-bearers to the *Westminster Confession,* and thus brought herself into line with the United Free Church. The climate for further Church union discussions had not yet been created, however, for the United Free Church could not easily reconcile herself to the idea of incorporation with a body that held the privileged position of State connection. Even as late as 1907 the Church and Nation Committee of the United Free Church sent a manifesto to the then Prime Minister, Sir Henry Campbell-Bannerman, urging upon the government the duty of disestablishing the Church of Scotland and stripping her of all endowments. Yet, in the following year, when the proposal was made by the Church of Scotland that the two Churches confer "in a friendly and generous spirit on the present ecclesiastical situation in Scotland" the suggestion was favourably entertained. Both Assemblies appointed large and influential committees, with Principal Alexander Martin as Clerk on the United Free side, and Dr John White in a similar capacity on the Church of Scotland. The first conference was held in the Goold Hall, Edinburgh, on 9th November 1909; and thus began the 20 years of discussion and negotiation which resulted in the great Church Union of 1929. The remit given by both Assemblies to their Committees was "to enter into unrestricted conference on the existing ecclesiastical situation, and on the main causes which kept the Churches apart."

It was evident from the outset that the way to Union was to be long and testing, and that much discussion and negotiation would be required before agreement could be ultimately reached.

147

The early determination of Dr John White to retain all that was distinctive of the Church of Scotland was expressed in a sermon which he preached in South Leith Church prior to his removal to the Barony parish of Glasgow in 1911. Claiming that the Church of Scotland had given full and practical proof of her desire for union, he declared, "I think she has gone as far as she need go. She must take her stand where she now is." These words, headlined in the press as "Established Church Ultimatum," were seized upon by opponents of Union, and had serious repercussions in the United Free Church. But Dr White had his way. His biographer, Augustus Muir, comments ". . . . the Church of Scotland did not move one inch on any fundamental matter from the position she took up in 1911. In all subsequent negotiations it was the United Free Church that moved step by step nearer to this position until at last the two Churches stood steadfastly together."[2]

In 1913 a sequence of *Articles Declaratory of the Church of Scotland in Matters Spiritual* was drawn up and discussed. These were largely the work of Dr White, and in their modified and finished form they were embodied in the ultimate Act of Parliament eight years later. These Articles increased the anxiety of the anti-Union party in the United Free Church, and Dr George Robson requested a clearer definition of the relations between Church and State that the Union Committee had in view. But Dr White's reply was uncompromising. Claiming that what Dr Robson desired would have the effect of bringing in a new danger, if acted upon, he asserted that "the respective spheres of civil and ecclesiastical courts had never been defined."[3] This, however, must be regarded as a piece of terminological jugglery; for, prior to the Disruption, the undivided Church of Scotland in its *Claim of Rights,* submitted as a last measure to avoid the breach with the State, had well defined the respective spheres of civil and ecclesiastical government as taught in Holy Scripture, and as formulated in the historic documents of the Reformed Church in Scotland and guaranteed by successive agreements between Church and State.

The 1914-18 War halted Union negotiations for a time, but by 1919 the *Declaratory Articles of the Church of Scotland in Matters Spiritual* were in shape to be sent down to the Presbyteries under the Barrier Act. The result was approval by an overwhelmingly large majority, and the next move was to ask Parliament to embody the Articles in an Act which would be preparatory to Union.

When the Bill "for facilitating the Church Union in Scotland" was presented to Parliament in April 1921 it was immediately opposed by sympathisers with the minority in the United Free Church who were critical of the Union measures. Mr Tom Johnston, M.P., urged that the Bill be dropped until the government showed its hand over what would be done with the teinds and endowments. The Hon. Alexander Shaw charged the Union leaders with insincerity. The Bill, he said, had been presented in one way to the Church of Scotland, and to the United Free Church in another. The former Church had been told that she would be Established more firmly than ever, while the latter had been assured that the Bill was really equivalent to dis-Establishing the Church of Scotland. But it passed without a division, and with similar ease made its way through the House of Lords. Having secured Parliament's consent to her Articles, the Church's next step was to have a Bill introduced that would give her power over her own endowments.

The lesson of the Free Church Appeal of 1904 had not been forgotten. Anxious to avoid the contract with the State which is at the root of all civil endowment, the Union planners were determined to retain such coverage for the Church's acceptance of the *Confession* as would enable her to change her doctrine as the whims of the passing years might require. She wanted endowment, with the liberty to do with it very much as she pleased.

At this stage, the intransigent Voluntaries, led by Rev. James Barr, made every effort to stall proceedings. Barr had formed a United Free Church Association which served as a rallying-centre for those who objected mainly on Voluntary grounds, to the Union.

The debate on the second reading of the Bill took place on February 10th, 1925. The opposition were ably led by Barr, now Labour M.P. for Motherwell, and by Rosslyn Mitchell, Labour M.P. for Paisley, and legal adviser to the United Free Church Association. Both attacked the Burgh Grants, the Exchequer Grants and Teinds as conferring an advantage upon the Church of Scotland that was unfair to other Churches, and that imposed an unjustifiable burden on people not connected with the Establishment. But the Bill went through, and when it reached the Scottish Grand Committee, Dr John White was given a seat in the Committee Room, so as to be at hand when questions were raised—a position which he used with his utmost skill in the interests of Union.

In this connection, reference must be made to assurances given by Dr White regarding Free Church participation in the patrimony of the Church of Scotland.

The Free Church of Scotland, in accordance with her *Claim of Rights,* had always asserted her entitlement to a share in the patrimony. She had come out from the Establishment in 1843 on the Establishment Principle, holding unyieldingly to the contract between Church and State as set forth in the Revolution Settlement of 1690. Her claim could not be lightly dismissed. The original contract of 1690 was being virtually annulled by the 1925

149

legislation, for the substitute contract was based upon the Declaratory Articles of 1921. The Free Church was discharging her duties under the original contract, although no longer participating in the material benefits of Establishment. It seemed to her a reasonable expectation that her *Claim of Rights* should be considered afresh, now that the patrimony of the Church of Scotland was to be pooled, and thereafter administered by a board of Commissioners. Her right to participate in the Exchequer Grants in particular seemed indisputable.

These Grants originated in Acts of Parliament which were passed in 1823 and 1824, setting apart £50,000 for the building of additional churches with manses in the Highlands and Islands. These Parliamentary Churches, as they were known, received £120 from the National Exchequer in respect of stipend. By another Act, revising an Act of 1810, there were 206 parishes in receipt of Exchequer Grants, so as to increase the stipend to £150. Altogether, there was an annual endowment of £17,000 from the National Exchequer in this connection.

The making of this provision was regarded by some as being a measure of redress by the State for the large annual sum that had been diverted to the Crown from the revenues of the Scottish Church at the Reformation. At all events, the Grants were intended to help with the maintaining of the Church's ministry in the Highland area.

At the Disruption the large majority of the people in the parishes favoured by these Grants identified themselves with the Free Church of Scotland, leaving only very small remnants adhering to the Church of Scotland. Now that the Church's patrimony was to be pooled, and administered by a board of Commissioners, it seemed but just and equitable, that the Free Church should—seeing that to all intents and purposes she was doing the work of the parish church in many of those areas—be regarded as having a just claim to the provision that had been made there for the maintenance of Gospel ordinances.

Accordingly, the Free Church Law Agent, Sir James Simpson, arranged a conference in Glasgow with Dr John White, and was accompanied, at his own request, by Professor J. Kennedy Cameron, and Professor Donald Maclean. The quotations which follow are from a narrative of proceedings compiled by Sir James Simpson, and attested as correct by the two professors.

Sir James Simpson's proposals were that, "inasmuch as all the patrimony of the Church of Scotland was now to be pooled, and administered by a selected Board of Commissioners: (1) where we were able to fulfil the conditions of these endowments, and where the strength of the Church of Scotland did not justify a continued ministry, except as a sectarian witness, we should be given a share of those grants; (2) that a clause should be added to the Bill to make this proposal effective; (3) that if it was impossible to endow us directly from the State, we should accept such grants through the proposed Commissioners; (4) that a Committee of the Churches interested should be appointed to delimit territories for each Church, having regard to numbers, and to local wishes, in harmony with such financial arrangements.

"Dr White replied: (1) that historically and ecclesiastically, we in the Free Church were entitled to the share of the Exchequer Grants indicated; (2) that he could not undertake to introduce a clause into the Bill, as other claimants, especially Roman Catholics, might come forward. He solemnly promised, however, that if we allowed the Bill to pass without opposition, he would, once the pooled funds were in the possession of the Church, create a joint-committee that would at once distribute these Exchequer funds in the way indicated by us; and (a) that as this was purely a matter between the Church of Scotland and the Free Church, whatever numbers of the United Free Church might afterwards enter into the Church of Scotland in the Highland area they would not be taken into reckoning when the financial adjustments were being made; and (b) that the Committee would delimit areas, remove the scandal of unnecessary churches, and smooth the feeling between Churches, subject always to the authority of their respective judicatories. Dr White, finally, most generously offered and promised that, in the event of his failing to secure for us from his Church a share of these Grants, he would himself, as a token of his Church's gratitude to the Free Church for its anti-disestablishment services in the 'eighties of last century, collect a fund up to £30,000 as an equivalent of these grants. Dr Maclean respectfully warned him that he thought the Free Church might not care to become a beneficiary of the Church of Scotland for what it conceived to be a service of conscience. Nevertheless, Dr White persisted in his generous promise.

"Accepting these promises as sincerely given, the Free Church withdrew their opposition to the Bill. Mr Ian Macpherson, M.P. (afterwards Lord Strathcarron), was written to, and asked to obtain from Sir John Gilmour, the Secretary for Scotland, a guarantee that the generous promises given by Dr White would be implemented by the Church of Scotland. As the world knows, the Secretary for Scotland gave that assurance on the floor of the House of Commons."[4]

The account that is given by Augustus Muir of the above discussions, in his biography of Dr John White, is biased and misleading in the extreme. He omits all mention of Professors Maclean and Kennedy Cameron, and merely states that Dr White

151

"had to face the Law Agent of the Free Church over a demand for a money grant in northern districts where the 'Wee Frees' claimed they predominated." "Two Church of Scotland ministers in the North made careful enquiries," he adds, "and reported to John White that the claim of the 'Wee Free' leaders that their Church was doing the work of a National Church had no foundation in fact. The Free Church Law Agent then (according to Muir), bowed his head and withdrew his claim, and so John White spared the Standing Committee from yet another wrangle."[5]

An extract from a footnote that Muir appends to his narrative of this incident ties up more easily with Sir James Simpson's record than it does with the account given by Muir, for it reads (and it is a quotation from Dr White, following a kindly reference by him to the good work of the Free Church in some of the areas covered by the Exchequer Grants), "After legislation has been passed, one would hope that a conference between the Churches would be possible, and that this would lead to some better and less wasteful methods of supplying religious ordinances in many parishes than are in use at present."[6]

But the legislation was passed, and the neighbourly promises of earlier days were forgotten. Many in the Free Church deplored the withdrawal of opposition to the Bill, maintaining that the Church's duty was to press her *Claim of Rights,* whatever might come of it. The attraction of the more peaceful method was strong, however, and it could well be argued that in pressing her *Claim of Rights* at a Church Conference the Free Church would not be less faithful to her trust than she would have been by pressing it before Parliament. But the Conference was never held.

After the passing of the Properties and Endowments Act in 1925, the Church of Scotland enacted her *Articles Declaratory* and proceeded to prepare the basis of Union on which it was planned to bring the two Churches together.

There was still an understandable uneasiness in the United Free Church regarding what were euphemistically called "the vestiges of Establishment" that would still remain in the Church after the 1929 Union, and great pains were taken to play these down. Dr R. J. Drummond of Edinburgh, in a speech delivered in the United Free Church General Assembly as late as 1928, acknowledged that there were some in that Church who were unwilling "to participate in any way in funds for ministerial support derived from what were formerly the teinds."[7] But, apart from endowment, the idea of State connection of any kind was repugnant to them. After so recently campaigning for the dis-establishment of the Church of Scotland their entering upon Union with an Established Church would require a great deal of explaining.

To do this the more effectively, the Law Committee of the Church consulted with the Rt. Hon. H. P. Macmillan, K.C. (afterwards Lord Macmillan), and Mr Oswald Dykes, K.C., Professor of Law at Edinburgh University, and obtained reassuring answers to their questions. Nowhere, said these legal advisers, did the *Articles Declaratory of the Church of Scotland* lay down that "it is an article of faith of the Church that the State has the right and duty to support an establishment of religion."[8] And, as for the endowments, the fact that, by the Act of 1925, the Church of Scotland now held its patrimonial rights in entire independence of the State should be regarded as settling the matter once and for all.

The line of reasoning followed is marked by a naivete that one does not easily associate with eminent jurists, and it gives rise to the impression that the legal authorities consulted were at pains to give their clients the strongest support possible for the views of the situation which the pro-union party were circulating throughout the Church. But it was a weak argument that the mere transference of the function of administering the patrimony, from the State to a body of ecclesiastical commissioners, so radically changed the character of the funds involved that the patrimonial benefits could now be accepted without scruple by even the most perfervid Voluntaries. Lest, however, there should still be some congregations to whom the argument did not carry conviction, it was provided that they might "dissociate themselves from any share in the funds referred to."

Furthermore, ecclesiastical politics were all too evident in the view that the remaining "vestiges of State connection" were too insignificant to be of any real account. Is the pledge of special recognition and support of the National Church, exacted from the Sovereign at his or her coronation, of so little significance that it can lightly be set aside in this way? And has the presence of the Lord High Commissioner—the Sovereign's representative—at the Assembly so lost its meaning that it has become a mere "vestige" of Establishment? Even when he brought the monarch's message which expressed (as it still continued to do after the 1929 Union) his "determination to maintain at all times Presbyterian Church Government in Scotland?" The office itself is statutory, and can be abolished only by specific Parliamentary legislation.

Remembering the House of Lords judgment of 1904, to the effect that because she had departed from the constitution of the Free Church of Scotland, the United Free Church could not fall heir to the Free Church patrimony, the Law Committee of the United Free Church desired reassurances that their Church by uniting with the Church of Scotland in terms of the Basis of Union presented, would carry with it into the Union its whole rights and property. Again the advice of their legal consultants was favourable. But there is something more than a faint echo of the 1904 judgment in the reminder of counsel that "Without some nucleus of fundamental doctrine a competent trust cannot exist in the eyes of the law," and that a departure from this agreed nucleus would be regarded legally as a breach of trust. It was a lesson learned in the school of affliction.

Altogether, it was a far cry from the intransigency of the old Voluntaries as represented by Principal George Hutton who, as Moderator of the United Free Church Assembly in 1926, broke with Church of Scotland and Free Church tradition by refusing to wear Court dress under his plain Geneva gown—this as a gesture of repudiation of the Establishment Principle!

The Union Assembly was held in October 1929, the Church of Scotland entering it without appreciable loss of membership, but the United Free Church leaving behind a minority among whom sincere Evangelicals were not lacking, but whose attitude to Union with the Church of Scotland was determined by their Voluntaryism rather than by any marked difference in doctrinal beliefs. Tribute was paid to them by their former brethren that they had accepted with such commendable charity the denuded position in which the Union left them, and had not created difficulties by pressing extravagant claims to property or trust funds. The fact was that no such course was open to them with any prospect of success. For, as already noted, the undivided United Free Church, in preparation for the transference to her of the portion of the funds and property that the weakened Free Church of Scotland could not fully use after 1900, had virtually annihilated the rights of minorities by her new legislation.

In her time of need the United Free Church Continuing (as the minority were for a time designated), found that she had thus actually disinherited herself by her involvement in that legislation. In the last Report of the Union Committee, however, it was proposed that £25,000 should be paid to the dissentient minority from the funds of the United Free Church as a full settlement of their financial interests. After a good deal of discussion this was accepted. It was also laid down as a guiding principle that where there was opposition to Union, congregational property and funds should go with the local majority; but the arrangement was not generally adhered to. Dr D. M. Forrester, as Moderator of the United Free Church Continuing Assembly in 1931, complained that "When on a vote taken in a congregation they (the Continuing Church), were found to be in a minority, they accepted the situation at whatever cost to their people concerned. When it was the other side that was found in a minority, they nevertheless had had too often to fight for well-nigh every inch of the ground."[9]

154

A number of people who had entered the Union of 1900 on the assurance that the Free Church Unionists would be taking the full testimony of the Free Church of Scotland with them, now had second thoughts about Church unions, and returned to the Church of their fathers, among them the large and warm-hearted congregation of Scalpay, Harris.

Dr Donald Maclean's comment in review of the surrender of principle shown by the United Free majority who entered the Church of Scotland is not unjust. "First of all," he writes, "their ecclesiastical theory of Voluntaryism vanished, when they, in their eagerness to recover Church property that was adjudicated not theirs, silently acquiesced in the action of the State, through Act of Parliament in 1905, conferring liberty to change its Formula on the State Church, and thus flagrantly contradicted their constantly repeated conviction that the only freedom the State should confer on the Church was the freedom of separation. In the second place, Voluntaryism on its practical side was immolated on the altar of necessity when the United Free Church accepted from the State, and under Royal Warrant, the patrimony of the Free Church."[10]

"Politics have much to do with it—I fear much more than religion;"—Dr Smeaton's pronouncement upon the earlier Church Union was equally applicable to the greater Union of 1929. Dr J. R. Fleming who wrote so enthusiastically about Scottish Church Union, admits this, at least in part. "No doubt," he writes in the review of events, "the political conditions were exceptionally favourable. Unionism had learned the lesson of compromise. Labour had but little interest in this kind of legislation, and did not trouble to oppose it. Independent Liberalism did not then count for much as a factor in debate."[11]

The mending of a breach in the structure of the Church ought to be an occasion when spiritual enlivenment would be much more in evidence than it was at the making of the breach. But it is a significant fact that in the Church Union of 1929 there was little trace of the pulsing life that marked the Free Church of Scotland when, in 1843, she parted company with the section of the Church of Scotland which elected to retain the benefits of establishment at the cost of her spiritual independence. The need in 1929 was for spiritual revival rather than structural union. To give priority to the latter is to miss the former; and structural union is not enough. "It is possible," writes Dr Samuel Chadwick, "to excel in mechanics and fail in dynamic. There is a superabundance of machinery; what is wanting is power. To run an organisation needs no God. Man can supply the energy, enterprise and enthusiasm for things human. The real work of a church depends upon the power of the Spirit."[12]

Let the Church turn Bible-wards again; let her proclaim again the message with which she has been put in trust and cease teaching for doctrines the commandments of men; let her kneel again at the feet of the crucified Lord saying, penitently and submissively, "Lord what wilt Thou have me to do?"; let her glory only in the Cross whose magnetism alone gathers all men unto Him, and the true unity of the Church will begin to appear. A Bible-based ecumenical movement would indeed be a God-given blessing in our day, but loyalty to the Word of God must always be the determining factor in all the proposals for that closer ecclesiastical communion that gives visibility to the essential unity of the Church in her glorified Lord. A true ecumenical relationship is unattainable on anything less.

1. G. Reith, *Reminiscences of the United Free Church Assembly*.
2. A. Muir, *John White;* p. 137.
3. ibid. p. 152.
4. *The Instructor;* May 1944.
5. A. Muir, *John White;* p. 136.
6. ibid. p. 240.
7. R. J. Drummond, *Lest We Forget;* p. 151.
8. ibid. p. 151.
9. J. Barr, *United Free Church of Scotland;* p. 212.
10. D. Maclean, *Aspects of Scottish Church History;* p. 137.
11. J. R. Fleming, *The Church in Scotland 1875-1929;* p. 107.
12. S. Chadwick, *The Way to Pentecost;* p. 15.

CHAPTER TWENTY

THE FREE CHURCH AND PRESBYTERIAN REUNION

All the compromises which have ever been made in the cause of God have always strengthened the enemy, done injury to the truth, enfeebled the weak, and were never to this day joined with a blessing.—*John Welsh.*

When the proposal for Union between the Church of Scotland and the United Free Church was mooted in 1908, Dr John White pressed that the invitation for inter-church conference should be extended to the Free Church also, although he well knew that the prospect of success in this case was remote indeed. Having so recently come through the fiery trial of the 1900 Union and its sequel, it was hardly to be expected that the Free Church would consider union conversations with the two larger Churches which, so recently, had virtually released themselves from their Confessional obligations and departed from standards and principles for the maintenance of which the Free Church minority had risked their all.

When in the following year John White reported on the replies of the Churches to the proposals for union conversations he summed up the result of the approach to the Free Church (according to Augustus Muir) in the one sentence: "The Wee Frees sent us a postcard to say NO."[1]

The reply from the Free Church was indeed a declinature of the invitation sent her, but the manner of its transmission was not by a postcard! The General Secretary no doubt followed the usual custom, which was, that when he received a communication that required action by a Standing Committee of the Church, he transmitted the letter to the Convener of the Committee concerned and sent a formal card of acknowledgement to the sender. This, presumably, is what happened in the case of the invitation referred to; but the postcard was not the end of the matter!

The Free Church gave all serious attention to the questions relating to further Union, and made various pronouncements upon them, eventually, in a circular issued in 1929, clearly indicating her reasons for not participating in the Church Union that was soon to take place.

"It would be the occasion of much joy to us, as Free Churchmen" — so runs the pamphlet — "to see the reunion of the sundered Presbyterians of Scotland on the ground held by our Reforming and Covenanting Fathers. It is a matter of sincere regret that we cannot regard the Union that is soon to be consummated as one that at all, worthily, answers such a description.

"In the Uniting Act which gives the basis of the intended Union there are mentioned, under the heading of General Constitution, as 'leading documents setting forth the constitution' of the united Church:—

1. United Free Church Act anent Spiritual Independence (1906).

2. Articles Declaratory of the Constitution of the Church of Scotland in Matters Spiritual (1926).

"The Spiritual Independence that is claimed in both these documents is not that which our Disruption Fathers claimed, but a revolutionary counterfeit which is divorced from a definite Constitution.

"Under the heading of Doctrine there are named, along with *The Westminster Confession of Faith* (1647):—

1. *United Presbyterian Church Declaratory Act* (1879).

2. *Free Church Declaratory Act* (1892), with *Act* (1894) relative thereto.

3. *Church of Scotland Act on the Formula* (1910).

"Thus the doctrine that is recognised as Standard in the projected Church is seriously at variance with the exhibition of the Reformed Faith, that has been historically, from the 17th to the 20th century, the Standard of the Church of Scotland."[2]

It was the chaotic position produced by the relaxation of Confessional teaching referred to that prompted Dr Neville Davidson of Glasgow, at the special sittings of the General Assembly, held in October 1960 to celebrate the 400th anniversary of the Scottish Reformation, to put forward a plea that an assembly of divines should meet, not this time in Westminster but in Edinburgh, "to examine Christian doctrine in the light of present-day knowledge." Pointing out that ministers and elders of the Church of Scotland were under obligation to declare general adherence to the *Westminster Confession*, he said that he was not unaware that they were given liberty of judgment in matters which did not enter into the substance of the faith. But who was to say what matters fell into this category? He confessed that he felt intellectually dishonest in this connection, and he pleaded that the Church be released from the "vague and ambiguous position of general adherence to a 17th century document, with endless loopholes for private judgment."

Dr Davidson made it clear that he himself did not hold to Confessional teaching in all matters. He was simply pleading for a return to more ethical ways in dealing with the Church's standards. For, indeed, to exact from an ordinand a pledge of loyalty to the doctrines which "enter into the substance of the faith," without signifying what these cardinal doctrines are, is to give him a charter as wide as the winds to preach almost anything he pleases, and to do so with the certainty that any theological aberrations to which he may give expression will not bring upon him any disciplinary measures at the hands of the courts of the Church. The purpose of the *Confession* as a bond of identity and as a defence against heretical teaching is in these circumstances completely nullified.

In his plea for a return to honesty in creed subscription Dr Davidson is to be commended, and it is possible to do this without sharing his views of Confessional teaching.

In recent years the question of the Church's future relation to the *Westminster Confession* has been much under discussion in the various Courts of the Church of Scotland. It was proposed that it should be demoted from its time-honoured position as the principle subordinate standard of the Church, and relegated to the limbo of ancient documents and discarded creeds; an interesting museum piece, perhaps, but nothing more. Its replacement by a new statement of faith prepared by the Church's panel on doctrine was strongly urged, and agreed to, by a majority of Presbyteries. But when the matter came before the 1974 General Assembly the proposal was defeated by a narrow majority. Some voted for the retention of the *Confession* out of sincere loyalty to the Reformed position as systematised there. But many others did so from very different motives, preferring the condition of doctrinal confusion to which Dr Neville Davidson referred in 1960 to any specification of doctrines that must be regarded as entering into "the substance of the Faith." Thus the proposal that carried in the Assembly cannot by any stretch of the imagination be represented as a sign of returning orthodoxy. The most that can be said in its favour is that it has postponed for the time being the further demotion of the *Westminster Confession*, and has given the courts of the Church an opportunity to think again. We dare not claim for any formulation of the Faith that it represents the last word on all the subjects with which it deals; for that were to credit it with an authority which it does not, and was never meant to, possess. But the Church ought to be slow to revise a *Confession* such as was produced by the Westminster Divines, men of deep piety and profound scholarship, belonging to an age that was peculiarly suited to the formulation of sound doctrine and the systematising of the Church's faith and message.

The *Westminster Confession* inevitably reflects, in certain aspects, the situation of its own age, but it sets forth in masterly fashion the great truths of Divine revelation which belong to every age, and to which we must cling tenaciously if we are to retain our character as a Reformed Church. In the Scripture proofs which it adduces in support of the positions taken it frankly gives its Biblical authority for its definitions and postulates, so that it ought to be easy for the sincere enquirer to judge as to whether or not it diverges at any point from the teaching of the Word.

Creed examination would indeed be a laudable activity in the Church of today if the scrutineers were to follow the example of Scotland's early Reformers who, as John Row puts it, laid "God's Word before them and made reformation according thereunto, both in doctrine first, and then in discipline." The present-day anxiety to denote the *Westminster Confession,* however, only too obviously springs from a desire to be loosed from the complete subservience to the authority of Holy Scripture which the Confession demands, and is far removed from the spirit of our Scottish Reformers.

The Free Church of Scotland is not insensitive to the reproach of our divided Scottish Presbyterianism. She is neither sectarian nor isolationist. Although unable to participate in the Church Union of 1929, she unanimously, in her 1930 General Assembly, granted the crave of an overture which proposed the setting up of a Committee to confer with similar Committees which might be appointed by the Synods of the Reformed Presbyterian Church of Scotland, the United Original Secession Church, and the Free Presbyterian Church with a view to securing fuller co-operation between them, and, if possible, union. The Free Presbyterians declined even to confer, but the other denominations agreed, and several meetings were held between the representatives of these three denominations. Considerable progress had been made when the United Original Secession Church suddenly broke off negotiations, the ostensible reason being the failure to reach agreement on a suitable name for the enlarged Church in the event of Union. It had become increasingly apparent, however, that the trend in the Secession Church was more in the direction of the Church of Scotland, with which body they eventually united in 1956. The Secession congregation of Kilwinning, long served by the Rev. Thomas Matthew — a true son of the Erskines — chose rather to make affinity with the Free Church. Other Secession congregations simply disbanded, some office-bearers and several members making their new home with the Free Church.

Negotiations with the Reformed Presbyterians ended at that point, but were resumed at their request, in 1966, when the Free Church General Assembly readily agreed to appoint a Committee to confer with them. Again several meetings were held, as a result of which a fuller understanding was reached of the respective positions and circumstances of the two denominations. There was no decision to unite, but ways of fuller co-operation were discussed and agreed upon, and the cordial relations already existing were strengthened.

The Free Church has, all along, shown her readiness to co-operate in every way possible with other evangelical denominations, especially those that belong to the Reformed family. She has been a constituent member of the Reformed Ecumenical Synod almost from the founding of that body. Her willingness to co-operate in the fullest possible way with Evangelicals who are outside the strictly Reformed circle is evident from her membership of the British Evangelical Council. On moral and social matters she co-operates, without compromise of distinctive testimony, with all the Protestant Churches in Scotland. In these and other ways she endeavours to be worthy of the honoured name that she bears, and true to the cherished tradition of the Free Church of Scotland.

"John Knox's gospel is my gospel," declared C. H. Spurgeon, during the Down-Grade Controversy in the Baptist Union. "That which thundered throughout Scotland must thunder through England again." Yes, and we add, "through Scotland again." And we hold to the faith of our fathers believing that God will still be working His miracles of grace and salvation by that Gospel when all the spurious gospels devised by the mind of man have finally been swept out to the scrap-heap to which they are destinated.

The concluding paragraph of the pamphlet issued in 1929 by the Free Church Claim of Right Committee is still good counsel for Free Church people. It says: "As Free Churchmen we are called upon to stand fast and hold our ground. Ours is the unvitiated Constitution of the old Reformed Church in Scotland. We have no need to apologise for our fulness of doctrinal profession nor for the simplicity of our New Testament worship. A mighty tide of spiritual revival would bring our drifting brethren back to the mooring-ground of our fathers. This would make it possible for a union to be brought about, such as would, in prospect, have rejoiced the hearts of our Reforming, Covenanting and Disruption worthies. For such a consummation we are called upon to work and pray. It would 'turn the hearts of the fathers to the children, and the disobedient to the wisdom of the just'."

For "such a consummation" let us indeed "work and pray."

1. A. Muir, *John White;* p. 14.
2. *The Free Church and the Union Movement; Claim of Right Committee;* pp. 1, 2.

CHAPTER TWENTY-ONE

THE FREE CHURCH IN THE WORLD OF TODAY

The Word of God is quite sufficient to interest and bless the souls of men throughout all time; but novelties soon fail—*C. H. Spurgeon.*

It has become common to regard the Free Church of Scotland, and other denominations like her that have held to Reformed doctrine and worship throughout a century of change as bodies that have fallen out of the march of theological and ecclesiastical progress, and that are destined on that account to pass speedily into oblivion. It was this belief that led Principal Rainy in 1900 to allow the Free Church a mere five years of survival. But it is surely in the good purpose of God that this Church is still in action, and that, despite shifts of population from areas where her congregations are principally located, and the toll taken by emigration to lands abroad, as well as the general decline in spiritual life everywhere, her pulse is still steady. And, unlike a Stewart king of unhappy memory, she has no cause to apologise for being "so unconscionable a time in dying." She still has work to do, and is immortal until it is done.

There are many indeed who express the view that, as a distinct denomination, her work should be regarded as already finished, and that her future contribution to the Christian good of Scotland depends on her readiness to accommodate herself to the changed world of today, and take her place in the national Church of Scotland, as those who left the Establishment before her have already done.

In his book, *The Church in Changing Scotland,* A. H. Dunnett writes of a visit which he paid to a community in Skye where he found a "multiplicity of churches," with a rigidity of denominational loyalty which he deplores. The cause of this exclusiveness he finds in the people concerned. "The highlander," he says, "never looks forward. He lives essentially in the past." He credits the Free Church of Scotland with having two-thirds of the people in the locality referred to, and he finds "nothing distinctive about its teaching to prevent unity with the other churches. But its people will have little or nothing to do with the Church of Scotland because the memory of the hardness of the Disruption still remains."

According to this view—and it is widely propagated—there is no longer any justification for the separate existence of the Free Church of Scotland. Patronage, which was so largely responsible for the fragmentation of Scottish Presbyterianism, is no longer a live issue, and the way to reunion is clear. The time has come for the Free Church to end her separate witness!

Statements made by her great Disruption leader, Dr Thomas Chalmers, are sometimes quoted against her. Did he not say in his Moderatorial address in the Tanfield Hall. "We quit a vitiated Establishment, but would rejoice in returning to a pure one"? The Patronage Act of 1874 purged the Establishment of the old evil of patronage; what justification then could there be for continuing the Free Church? Furthermore, we are reminded that as early as December 1844 Chalmers had publicly expressed his disregard for mere denominationalism in the exclamation, "Who cares for the Free Church?" And Principal Hugh Watt sees his "radiant figure" at the Union Assembly of October 1929, "dwarfing all other intrusions from the past, raising those speaking hands of his in benediction. . . ."[1]

But is this a reliable picture that Dr Watt presents? Or is the historian for once, like Sheridan's "Right honourable gentleman", indebted to his imagination for his facts?" Let us see.

To begin with, did the Church of Scotland become, by the Patronage Act of 1874, the "pure Establishment" to which Chalmers said the Free Church would "rejoice" to return? Would that legislation have satisfied him? To this question at least, we have his own answer in advance. Speaking in the City Hall, Glasgow, in March 1843, he declared: "The abolition of Patronage will not satisfy us; we must have an independent power of discipline; we must have an independent jurisdiction in things ecclesiastical."

Can it be claimed that the 1874 Act fulfilled these conditions? The Duke of Richmond who introduced the Bill, quite plainly asserts that it did not. "We have been astonished," he says, "to find it stated that the Bill did away with Patronage altogether." And Sir Henry Wellwood Moncrieff, in his Chalmers' Lectures, 1883, enumerates various limitations of jurisdiction to which the Church of Scotland was still subject — limitations which proved that her spiritual independence was not yet as complete as Chalmers and his contemporaries would have demanded. Another ecclesiastical authority, Professor William Milligan D.D., of Aberdeen University, publicly warned his Church of Scotland brethren that no Union could be looked for between the Church of Scotland and the Free Church on the ground of the Patronage Act of 1874, because the Free Church held a principle which the Establishment had rejected, viz., the independence of the Church in spiritual matters.

There were many who held that just as the Act of Queen Anne in 1712 was Erastian in imposing Patronage upon the Church, so too was the Act of 1874 in removing it. For, basically, both Acts did the same thing in that they treated the appointment of ministers in the Church as a civil right which the State has the power to bestow on whom it will. In 1712 Parliament bestowed that right on the patrons; in 1874 Parliament bestowed it upon the people, nominally at least.

The Free Church Synod of Fife expressed precisely this view in a Resolution which it adopted shortly after the passing of the 1874 Patronage Act. The Resolution says: "That as Patronage was not the cause of the Disruption, the abolition of Patronage cannot by itself open the way for the reunion of the Free and Established churches. Still less can this be accomplished by the Act of last session of Parliament, which does not prohibit patronage, but hands over the civil right to be exercised by a new class of persons."[2]

A similar judgment was set before the Jubilee Assembly of the Free Church in 1893 when the Moderator, Dr W. C. Smith, alluding to the view that the way was now open for the return of the Free Church to the Establishment, said, "It is no pleasure to us to see any part of the Church of Christ hampered by external interference. But as to the proposal that we should now return to the Church which has got nearly all we once asked, that is a very different matter. For one thing, its freedom has not been recognised as the inalienable right of the Church of Christ — it has only been granted as a boon which meanwhile it was safe for the Church to bestow, and which also it might be right at another time to recall. . . . We cannot accept as a boon what we hold to be our birthright and heritage in Him."[3]

But even if it be accepted that the 1874 Act *did* effectively remove the old cause of estrangement between the Church of Scotland and the Free Church, is it conceivable that, for the sake of ecclesiastical reunion, Chalmers would have regarded with complacency the compromises over Confessional doctrine that were agreed upon by the uniting parties in order to make possible the reunions of 1900 and 1929?

Again let us return to the Tanfield Hall and listen as he expounds the manifesto of the Free Church of Scotland. Commending his brethren on their decision to suffer the loss "of everything that is dear to nature" rather than run counter to "the Bible, our Great Church Directory and Statute Book," he urges them to follow the example of "the first teachers of Christianity" who, in all things, made their way by the light of God's unerring Word. "They had indeed the voice of inspiration," he adds, "and why may not we do the same, who walk by no light, and submit

164

to no authority in spiritual things, but the light and authority of the enduring book, the Bible — the common statute book for both ministers and people. Certain it is that the apostles, who said they would obey God rather than man, carried this principle into effect whether the men were many or few; and so at one time we find them in favour with all the people, become in many instances the objects of popular dislike and violence."[4]

That then was Chalmers' thought of the Bible and its place in the government of the Church. Christ was Head and King of the Church, and the Holy Scriptures were the Statute Book and Directory of His realm. Chalmers saw, and his associates in the Evangelical Party saw with him, that the Church does not properly honour Christ, her King, if she at any time refuses to recognise the absolute authority of Holy Scripture. The slogan, "Not the Bible but Christ" so widely used towards the end of last century, bears the brand of its own illogicality. For, as Dr A. Moody Stuart so clearly pointed out in a speech before the Free Church Presbytery of Edinburgh in this period of doctrinal change, "We know nothing of Christ except what we read in the Bible, and when it is discredited, men can have no Christ except by their own conception. The authority of both is supreme. We have both, or we have neither."

It requires a great stretch of imagination, and something more, to associate the Evangelical leader, Thomas Chalmers, whose sermons, they said, were "the Bible in solution," with the Union Committee who drew up the *Articles Declaratory* on which the Church Union of 1929 was carried through.

When it is argued that Dr Chalmers was no narrow denominationalist the point is immediately conceded. But when his remark, made in December 1844, "Who cares for the Free Church?" is used against those who continue the Free Church of Scotland today, fairness requires that the words be related to their context.

The quotation is taken from an address which he delivered in Edinburgh in the interests of the working classes who were neglected in the provision of churches and schools, and his aim was to show that this was not a denominational enterprise. "Some people say," he declared, "'Oh, this is all a scheme of the Free Church'. Now, I say, this is a mistake. *Who cares about the Free Church compared with the Christian good of the people of Scotland? Who cares for any Church, but as an instrument of Christian good?"* Who indeed? Thomas Chalmers speaks for the Free Church of Scotland still.

The Free Church of today can claim in sincerity that like Chalmers and his co-adjutors in 1843, she takes no pleasure in denominationalism for its own sake. Like them she would rejoice in the healing of ecclesiastical divisions and the sweetening of ecclesiastical relationships. These unhappy divisions are usually the fruit of doctrinal laxity and error; and, this being so, the first step towards a reunion must obviously be, as Chalmers indicated, the removal of the particular "vitiation" that caused the breach in the first place. Dialogue let there be; but if it is to serve its avowed purpose there must also be a final arbiter to decide the issue. "To the law and to the testimony:" cried Isaiah, "if they speak not according to this word, it is because there is no light in them." (Is. 8: 20). This watchword of long ago was adopted by the Reformers and used on many historic occasions. It assumed that there is one standard of truth, one ultimate authority to which men ought to carry their appeal in spiritual problems, and we have this ultimate oracle in the Holy Scriptures. "The Supreme Judge, by which all controversies of religion are to be determined," wrote the Westminster Divines, "and all decrees of councils, opinions of ancient writers, doctrines of men and private spirits, are to be examined, and in whose sentence we are to rest, can be no other but the Holy Spirit speaking in the Scripture."[5]

It is sometimes objected against this Confessional view that it fails to attach sufficient weight to the fact that the Holy Spirit speaks through the living Church as well as through the written Word. But the obvious answer to this objection surely is that — as Knox reminded Queen Mary — "the Holy Ghost is never contrarious to Himself." If there should be a contradiction between what He says in the Word, which "endureth for ever," and what He is alleged to be saying through the consciousness of the Church, then it is the latter communication that comes under suspicion and requires to be tested. And if on comparison it fails to come through the test of Holy Scripture it must be rejected as spurious. Thomas Carlyle's dictum is fully apposite to our own times. Referring to the new prophets that were emerging, he calls upon them to examine anew their credentials. "The prophet says, 'Thus saith the Lord.' Yes, Sir, but what if it be not the Lord, but only you who take your own fancies for the Word of the Lord?"

A return to the dogmatic theology of Evangelical Christianity is a prime prerequisite of a revived Church and an enlightened people. The true ecumenicity is unity in the faith of the Evangel. Referring to modern efforts toward church unity, Peter H. Eldersveld speaks of them as being, for the most part, "founded upon a minimum of Truth, the lowest possible common denominator of faith, the few points of doctrine on which there can be complete agreement," and adds, "but when you exclude all the great truths in historic Christianity on which there has been controversy, you are robbing the Church of most of the important things that Jesus taught us. And then you will not get a Church that comes as close as possible to being a manifestation of Him, but rather one that looks least like Him. That kind of broad and all-comprehensive unity will mean very little in the effort to bring the whole Gospel to the world."[6]

The doctrinal permissiveness of modern ecumenism aims at making an end of all heresy by the simple expedient of blurring all standards of orthodoxy. The particularist view of the Atonement can be proclaimed alongside the universalist view. Indeed, the atoning nature of our Lord's death on the Cross can be affirmed or denied in the same fellowship. Ecumenical eschatology can express or deny belief in a final judgment, in heaven and hell, in conditional or unconditional immortality. The pooling of these beliefs is advocated apparently without any awareness of incongruity. The churches' creeds are so adapted as to make them appear to sanction what, on appeal to the authority of Holy Scripture, they once clearly rejected. External and organisational unity may thereby be advanced; but the "unity" thus reached will constantly have to be under repair, and will never truly represent that unity for which our Lord prayed in His High Priestly intercession. The sanctified unity in the Truth which He there seeks for His people is as different from the eclecticism of the modern Liberal ecumenist as day is from night. And history clearly reveals that the greatest periods in our Scottish Church life were those in which the Reformed theology, as formulated in our Standards, was in the ascendancy. Intellectual, as well as moral and spiritual, progress was then in clearest evidence among the people. "The Reformed religion," affirms Ian Finlay in an attractive study of Scottish religious and cultural development, "prepared the way for all the Scottish philosophers and scientists." Where there has been spiritual revival it has always been through a return to the cardinal verities of Biblical Theology. "The victories of Christianity," writes that eminent Evangelical of the English Church, Dr J. C. Ryle, "wherever they have been won, have been won by distinct doctrinal theology; by telling men of Christ's vicarious death and sacrifice; by showing them Christ's substitution on the cross, and His precious blood; by teaching them justification by faith and bidding them believe on a crucified Saviour; by preaching ruin by sin, redemption by Christ, regeneration by the Spirit; by lifting up the brazen serpent; by telling men to look and live — to believe, repent and be converted. This is the only teaching which for eighteen centuries God has honoured with success, and is honouring at the present day both at home and abroad."

And Bishop Ryle's estimate is as accurate today as it was a century ago when it was first made. The testimony to which the

Free Church of Scotland, and all who stand with her in the Reformed succession, are pledged is a banner given by God to them that fear Him that it may be displayed because of the truth. The banner is stained with blood, not only the blood of our honoured martyrs, but the blood of Him Who trod the winepress alone. Today its supporters are few; tomorrow (and pray God the dawn may not be long delayed), it shall rally the forces of a revived Church and lead them to victory.

"He shall see of the travail of His soul, and shall be satisfied." And in all things He shall have the pre-eminence.

The battle is still on. His Church has had her grievous reverses, and shall continue to sustain setbacks until it pleases the Captain of her salvation to arise and plead His own cause. But

> *Freedom's Battle once begun,*
> *Bequeathed by bleeding sire to son,*
> *Tho' baffled oft, is ever won.*

Therefore "let us hold fast the profession of our faith without wavering; for He is faithful that promised."

1. H. Watt, *Thomas Chalmers and the Disruption;* pp. 358, 359.
2. W. Wood, *The Free Church and the Patronage Act;* p. 49.
3. *Proceedings of Free Church Assembly 1893;* p. 7.
4. ibid. 1843; p. 10.
5. *Westminster Confession of Faith;* Ch. 1, Section 10.
6. P. Eldersveld, *That Ye May Believe;* p. 154.

INDEX